# Quick & Easy Sushi Cook Book

**Distributors:**

**UNITED STATES:** Kodansha America, Inc., through Oxford University Press, 198 Madison Avenue, New York, NY 10016

**CANADA:** Fitzhenry & Whiteside Ltd., 195 Allstate Parkway, Markham, Ontario L3R 4T8

**UNITED KINGDOM AND EUROPE:** Premier Book Marketing Ltd., Clarendon House, 52, Cornmarket Street, Oxford, OX1 3HJ England

**AUSTRALIA AND NEW ZEALAND:** Bookwise International, 174 Cormack Road, Wingfield, SA 5013 Australia

**JAPAN:** Japan Publications Trading Co., Ltd., 1-2-1, Sarugaku-cho, Chiyoda-ku, Tokyo, 101-0064 Japan

# FOREWORD

Since Japan is surrounded by the sea, it is no wonder that its people consume large quantities of seafood. Their diet has always depended heavily on seafood, which can explain their leading position in the world longevity charts for the last 20 years. Japanese people live to 80 years of age on average, and it is now known that this is due in large part to the fact that nutrients from seafood prevent circulatory and other lifestyle-related diseases. Partly for this reason, Japanese cuisine is attracting worldwide interest, which I am very pleased to see.

Seafood is eaten in many ways across the country. Among the various methods of preparation, the healthiest (by which I mean low in calories) and popular style is called "*sashimi*" - that is, fresh fish served au naturel. A variety of fish and shellfish are cut into various bite-sized forms such as cubes, threads, and paper-thin slices, and then dipped into a mixture of soy sauce and *wasabi* at the table.

*Sashimi* pressed onto vinegared rice is known as *sushi*, or to be precise, *edomae-zushi*, which means Tokyo-style *sushi*. Other *sushi* dishes include combinations with cooked seafood and vegetables, which are often mixed with or rolled in *nori* seaweed. This representative food of Japan has a long culinary history that dates back over a thousand years, when it was used as a way of preserving fish. According to records from the 10th century, seafood in brine was naturally fermented and then eaten as a preserved food. Later on, at the beginning of 17th century, cooked rice was added to accelerate this fermentation. *Sushi* as we know it today did not appear for another century, until the end of the Edo period.

During the course of its long history, many delightful *sushi* variations have been created, including *chirashi-zushi*, *inari-zushi*, *oshi-zushi*, and so on. As you may notice, *sushi* is pronounced "*zushi*" when added as a suffix to other words.

This book was written to introduce this superb cuisine to those who would like to make it at home. Some of the recipes remain in their traditional form to retain their authenticity, while some have been adapted to satisfy more "modern tastes." The reader should feel free to leave out food that may be locally unavailable, and use instead any other ingredients that he or she sees fit. Also, the reader should know that there is no need to rigidly adhere to the rules of Japanese cuisine. The most important thing is to enjoy this fascinating yet simple style of cooking and entertaining from Japan.

*Yukiko Moriyama*

Tokyo
July 2002

# CONTENTS

## EDOMAE-ZUSHI

## PARTY SUSHI

## INFORMATION ON SUSHI

# INGREDIENTS

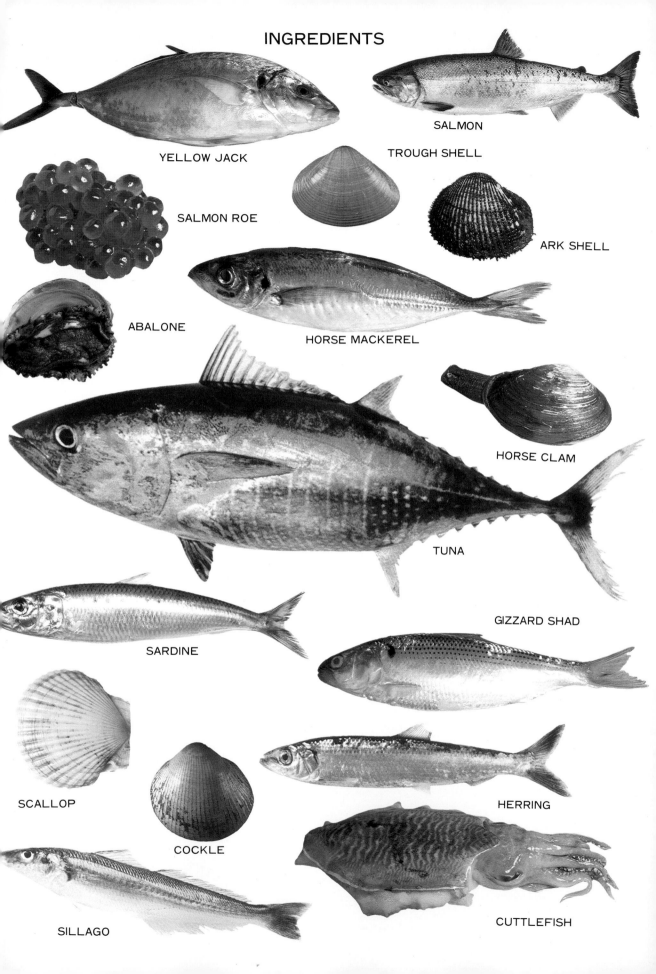

YELLOW JACK

SALMON

TROUGH SHELL

SALMON ROE

ARK SHELL

ABALONE

HORSE MACKEREL

HORSE CLAM

TUNA

GIZZARD SHAD

SARDINE

SCALLOP

COCKLE

HERRING

SILLAGO

CUTTLEFISH

# INGREDIENTS

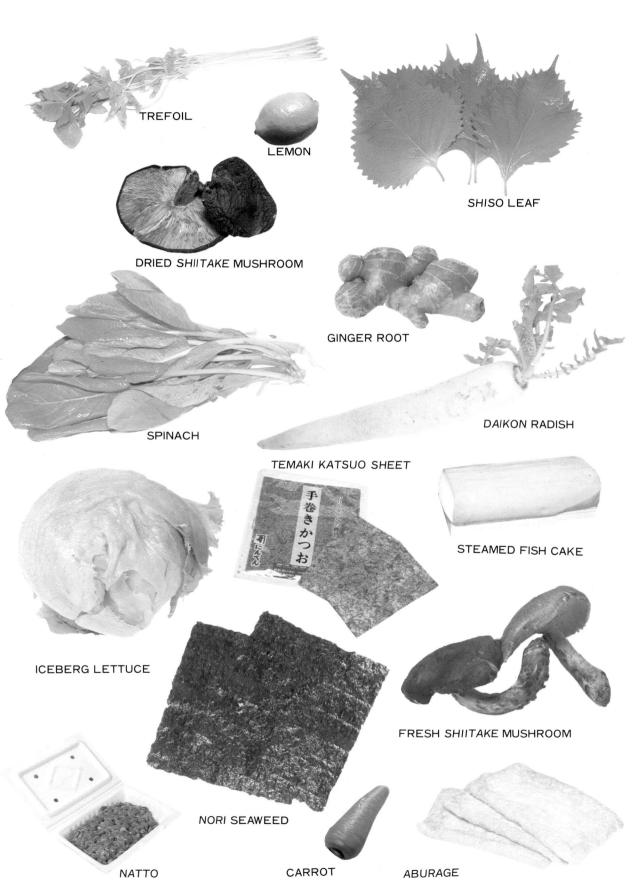

TREFOIL

LEMON

*SHISO* LEAF

DRIED *SHIITAKE* MUSHROOM

GINGER ROOT

*DAIKON* RADISH

SPINACH

*TEMAKI KATSUO* SHEET

STEAMED FISH CAKE

ICEBERG LETTUCE

FRESH *SHIITAKE* MUSHROOM

NORI SEAWEED

NATTO

CARROT

*ABURAGE*

# EDOMAE-ZUSHI

This is the fattiest part of the fatty tuna belly. It is light pink in color and melts in the mouth. Because it's the fattiest part of the tuna fish eaten raw, it's expensive and of course best eaten when in season (winter). Japanese people are very fond of it and for Westerners starting out on *sushi*, it's mildness and rich texture are guaranteed to bring you back for more.

## How To Prepare

① Cut off the reddest part (red tuna).

② Cut off the fattiest part.

③ Cut into long rectangular fillets, 1 in. (2.5 cm.) thick.

④ Cut diagonally across the lines into 1/8 in. (5 mm.) slices. (Slant the knife to the right, slice from the left end.)

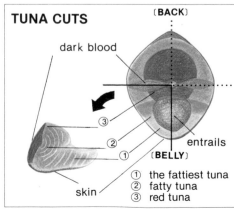

**TUNA CUTS**

〔BACK〕

dark blood

entrails

〔BELLY〕

③
②
①

① the fattiest tuna
② fatty tuna
③ red tuna

skin

Tuna is not sold whole but in cut offs. Each part of the tuna fish differs a lot in quality, and therefore in price. The fatty, pinkish part which is located close to the belly is called "toro". The lean, red part which is located close to backbone is called "akami". In the past, Japanese people put the highest value on *akami*, but as their tastes changed (after eating more meat in the Western way), *toro* took its place and became the most expensive.

## How To Shape *Sushi*

**INGREDIENTS: 2 fingers**

2 slices (about $\frac{1}{2}$ oz., 15 g. each) fattiest tuna
About $1\frac{2}{5}$ oz. (40 g.) *sushi* rice (See page 94-96)
Dash of *wasabi*

① Dip both hands into vinegared water (water:vinegar = 3:1). This prevents the rice from sticking to fingers.

② Take some rice in right fingers (about $\frac{2}{3}$ oz., 20 g.), hold gently and curl fingers to form oval.

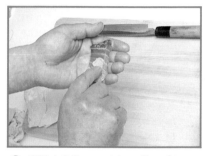
③ With left fingers, take a slice of tuna. Place a dab of *wasabi* in the center with right forefinger.

④ Lay the rice ball on fish.

⑤ With right forefinger, press the rice lightly down on fish.

⑥ Holding sides between thumb and forefinger, and curl left fingers over to right *sushi* so that fish is on top.

⑦ Press sides with right thumb and forefinger.

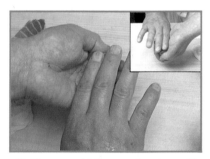
⑧ Shape *sushi* by pressing top with right fingers, and far end with left thumb.

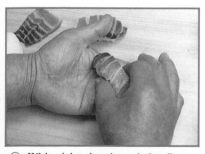
⑨ With right thumb and forefinger, turn *sushi* so that the other end can be shaped too.

⑩ Repeat as for ⑦.

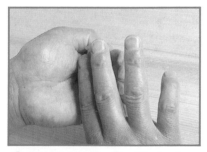
⑪ Repeat as for ⑧. Check shape again.

This is the moderately fatty part of the tuna belly. It's pink but not the faint pink of *ohtoro*. Again with the soft, butter-like feel of good tuna, combined with the sharp taste of *wasabi* (green horse-radish) and a touch of soy sauce, *chutoro* is a *sushi* must.

**How To Prepare**

① Cut off the reddest part (red tuna).

② Cut off the fattiest part. Now the fatty tuna is left. Cut into long rectangular fillets, 1 in. (2.5 cm.) thick.

③ Now the fillet is ready.

④ Cut diagonally into ⅛ in. (5 mm.) thick slices. (Slant the knife to the right and slice from the left end.)

⑤ The end pieces are triangular in shape. Slit from wide base and open out.

⑥ Opened out, ready as a topping.

### How To Shape *Sushi*

**INGREDIENTS: 2 fingers**

2 slices (about ¹/₂ oz., 15g. each) fatty tuna
About 1²/₅ oz. (40g.) *sushi* rice (See page 94-96)
Dash of *wasabi*

① Dip both hands into vinegared water (water: vinegar = 3:1). This prevents the rice from sticking to fingers.

② Take some rice in right fingers (about ²/₃ oz., 20g.), hold gently and curl fingers to form oval.

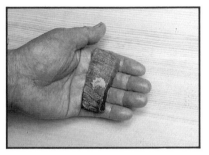

③ With left fingers, take a slice of tuna. Place a dab of *wasabi* in the center with right forefinger.

④ Lay the rice ball on fish.

⑤ With right forefinger, press the rice lightly down on fish.

⑥ Holding sides between thumb and forefinger, and curl left fingers over to right *sushi* so that fish is on top.

⑦ Press sides with right thumb and forefinger.

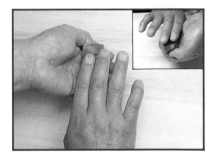

⑧ Shape *sushi* by pressing top with right fingers, and far end with left thumb.

⑨ With right thumb and forefinger, turn *sushi* so that the other end can be shaped too.

⑩ Repeat as for ⑦, ⑧.

⑪ Check shape again.

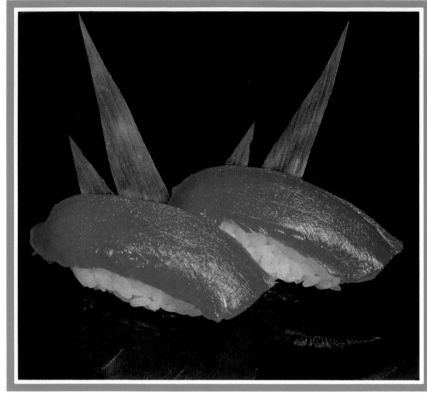

This is the lean meat near the spine of the tuna fish. It's various shades of red, with the lighter, shinier varieties being the best. For dieters however, the redder, the better. It's a part of every *sushi* meal and good for people trying raw fish for the first time; it's easy on the palate.

## How To Prepare

① Cut off the reddest part (red tuna).

② Cut into long rectangular fillets, each 1 in. (2.5 cm.) thick.

③ Cut diagonally into ⅛ in. (5 mm.) thick slices. (Slant the knife to the right, slice from the left end.)

④ The end pieces are triangular in shape. Slit from wide base and open out.

### TUNA AND SCIENCE

Ten years ago it was disclosed that the Eskimoes in Greenland rarely contracted heart or brain diseases in spite of their meat-eating customs. This led scientists to discover the "EPA", unsaturated fatty acid, in fish oil. Unsaturated fatty acid turns into two substances in your body; one which prevents the blood platelets from cohering, the other which enlarges the blood vessels to ease the blood flow.

Therefore eating a lot of fish containing this unsaturated fatty acid means taking precautions against hardening of the arteries or geriatric diseases. Fish that are supposed to be rich in this substance are tuna, yellowtail, sardines, etc... Fat from these fish contains around 10% of unsaturated fatty acid. And tuna contains another useful "DHA" that works the same as unsaturated fatty acid. Thus it has been proved that tuna "outshines" other fish, not only in its taste but also in its medicinal properties.

### How To Shape *Sushi*

**INGREDIENTS: 2 fingers**

2 slices (about ¹/₂ oz., 15g. each) red meat tuna
About 1²/₅ oz. (40g.) *sushi* rice (See page 94-96)
Dash of *wasabi*

① Dip both hands into vinegared water (water:vinegar=3:1). This prevents the rice from sticking to fingers.

② Take some rice in right fingers (about ²/₃ oz., 20g.) hold gently and curl fingers to form oval.

③ With left fingers, take a slice of tuna. Place a dab of *wasabi* in the center with right forefinger.

④ Lay the rice ball on fish. With right forefinger, press the rice lightly down on fish.

⑤ Holding sides between thumb and forefinger, and curl left fingers over to right *sushi* so that fish is on top.

⑥ Press sides with right thumb and forefinger. Shape *sushi* by pressing top with right fingers, and far end with left thumb.

⑦ With right thumb and forefinger, turn *sushi* so that the other end can be shaped too.

⑧ Repeat as for ⑥.

⑨ Check shape again.

### *SUSHI* AND BAMBOO LEAF

Bamboo leaf is closely connected to *sushi*, especially *nigiri-zushi*. Of course it makes an attractive decoration but it has other uses as well. First, bamboo leaf has a sterlizing and heat insulating effect. As they are high in salicylic acid and sulfurous acid, which are disinfectants, they keep the surface of raw fish free of bacterial growth. Also they prevent the rice or sauce from sticking to each other, so mixing colors or tastes. The contrast between black lacquer ware and white shiny rice decorated with fresh green leaves is attractive to look  at. Recently plastic bamboo leaves have become "popular". Although they are less expensive and handy, there are sound reasons for choosing to combine *sushi* and fresh bamboo leaves.

# 縞鯵 YELLOW JACK

This is yellow jack. It's one of the white *sushi* toppings. A slice of silvery *shima-aji* eaten with beef-steak plant and fresh ginger adds another taste to the *sushi* menu. The flavor is delicate and the texture of good (fresh) yellow jack is smooth and slides down easily.

## How To Prepare

① Wipe the surface with a wet cloth. Remove "hard scales" near the tail working from tail to head.

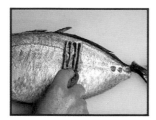

② Scrape off the scales.

③ Insert knife under pectral fin at the right angles, and make an incision toward pelvic fin in one motion.

④ Make a short slit in belly.

⑤ Remove head and entrails. Scrape out dark blood with knife.

⑥ Wash thoroughly under running water.

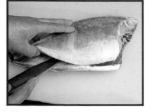

⑦ Insert knife under head and slice under-belly as far as backbone. Cut the back in the same way.

⑧ Cut off the tail. Cut the meat off from backbone.

⑨ Turn over, repeat ⑦ and ⑧.

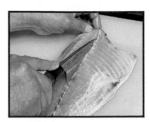

⑩ Insert knife under small bones along belly. When cutting, work knife at the right angles to fish.

⑪ Place the fish on board, skin side down. Divide into 2 fillets along the center line (Cut around bones, not through).

⑫ Cut off the center bones.

⑬ With skin side down, insert knife between skin and flesh in tail end. Pulling end of skin with left fingers, remove skin carefully.

⑭ Now the fillet is ready.

⑮ Slanting knife to the right, cut into ¹/₁₀ in. (3mm.) slices in one motion.

⑯ The end pieces are triangular in shape. Slit from wide base and open out.

## How To Shape *Sushi*

**INGREDIENTS: 2 fingers**

2 slices (about ³/₈ oz., 12g. each) yellow jack
About 1²/₅ oz. (40g.) *sushi* rice (See page 94-96)
Dash of *wasabi*

① Dip both hands into vinegared water (water: vinegar = 3:1). Take some rice (about ²/₃ oz., 20g.) and hold gently, Take a slice of yellow jack in left hand. With right forefinger, place *wasabi* in center.

② Lay the rice ball on fish. With right forefinger, press the rice lightly down on fish. This is to make the rice cling to fish.

③ Holding sides between thumb and forefinger, and curl left fingers over to right *sushi* so that fish is on top.

④ Press sides with right thumb and forefinger.

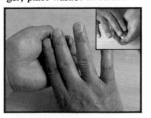

⑤ Shape *sushi* by pressing top with right fingers, and far end with left thumb.

⑥ With right thumb and forefinger, turn *sushi* so that the other end can be shaped too.

⑦ Repeat as for ④, ⑤. Check shape again.

# 鮃 FLOUNDER

This is flounder. Good *hirame* is a *sushi* gourmet's delight. Since it's cut from such a small part of the fish, it's scarce and expensive. In appearance it's pale pink and smooth, with no markings. It's best in December and January. The taste is delicate and buttery.

## How To Prepare

① Wipe surface well, scrape off scales using knife at a deep angle as flounder has fine, packed scales.

② Wash thoroughly. Make an incision at pectoral fin on both sides and cut along head.

③ Make a short slit in belly, remove head and entrails.

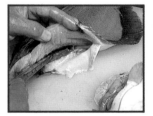

④ Scrape out entrails left and dark blood with knife.

⑤ Wash under running water.

⑥ Make an incision along fin.

⑦ Make an incision along the center line from head to tail.

⑧ Insert knife into incision and cut off the flesh free from the bone, from tail to head. (Filleting)

⑨ Be careful as flounder is fragile. Turn over. Cut off another fillet. Work the other side.

⑩ Now filleting is completed.

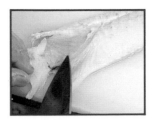

⑪ Slice off the small bones along belly. When cutting, change and cut at right angles to fish.

⑫ Cut off fins.

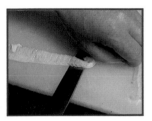

⑬ Place fish skin side down, insert knife at the tail between skin and flesh. Pulling the end of skin with left fingers, remove the skin.

⑭ Skinned, ready for slicing.

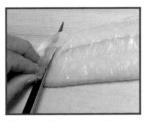

⑮ Cut into about ¹⁄₁₀ in. (3 mm.) thick slices. (Slant knife to the right and slice from the left end, thinly.)

⑯ Slices should be so thin you can see the knife through them. (White fish is tighter in texture than red fish. Thick slices are hard to chew, and spoil the taste.)

## How To Shape *Sushi*

**INGREDIENTS: 2 fingers**

2 slices (about ¹⁄₃ oz., 10 g. each) flounder
About 1²⁄₅ oz. (40 g.) *sushi* rice (See page 94-96)
Dash of *wasabi*

① Dip both hands into vinegared water (water : vineger = 3 : 1). Take some rice (about ²⁄₃ oz., 20 g.) and hold gently. Take a slice of flounder in left hand. With right forefinger, place *wasabi* in center.

② Lay the rice ball on fish, press down lightly with right forefinger. This is to make the rice cling to fish.

③ Holding sides between right thumb and forefinger, roll *sushi* over so that fish is on top.

④ Press sides with right thumb and forefinger.

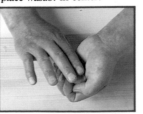

⑤ Shape *sushi* by pressing top with right fingers, far end with left thumb.

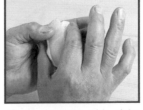

⑥ Turn *sushi* with right thumb and forefinger, so that the other end can be shaped too. Repeat as for ④.

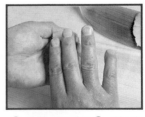

⑦ Repeat as for ⑤. Check shape again.

This is Japanese shad and a member of the herring family. It's a small silvergrey fish, with a black spotted back. Before it's served as *sushi*, it's marinated in vinegar and then the slice is crosshatched and placed on top of the *sushi* rice. The taste is strong and a firm favorite with herring fans.

## How To Prepare

① Soak in water before use. Remove the dorsal fin. Scrape off the scales from tail to head.

② Insert the knife behind black spots in head area, cut off the head.

③ Cut off underside of belly. Do not remove much meat.

④ Scrape out entrails.

⑤ Wash thoroughly.

⑥ Insert the knife in the belly, cut along backbone to open out.

⑦ Hold the fish, belly side down. Insert knife between flesh and bone at the head, remove the bone and tail.

⑧ Slice off small bones along belly. When cutting, work at right angles to fish.

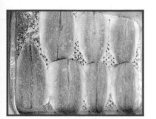

⑨ Sprinkle salt on bottom of shallow dish. (No metal) Put in fillets, skin side down. Sprinkle with salt and allow to set for about 30 min. to tighten the meat for a better taste.

⑩ Wash and drain in a drainer.

⑪ Marinate in vinegar, skin side down for about 10 min..

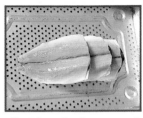

⑫ Discard vinegar and drain about 30 min..

⑬ Drained, ready to eat.

⑭ Cut off tail and hard part along dorsal fin.

⑮ Make a cross-cut incision in the skin.

⑯ Wave-cut incisions.

## How To Shape *Sushi*

**INGREDIENTS: 2 fingers**

**2 slices (about ¹/₂ oz., 15g. each) gizzard shad**
**About 1²/₅ oz. (40g.) *sushi* rice (See page 94-96)**
**Dash of *wasabi***

① Dip both hands into vinegared water (water:vinegar = 3:1). Take some rice (about ²/₃oz., 20g.) and hold gently. Take a slice of gizzard shad in left hand. With right forefinger, place *wasabi* in center.

② Lay the rice ball on gizzard shad, press down lightly with right forefinger. This is to make the rice cling to fish.

③ Holding sides between right thumb and forefinger, roll *sushi* over so that fish is on top.

④ Press sides with right thumb and forefinger.

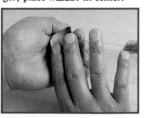

⑤ Shape *sushi* by pressing top with right fingers, far end with left thumb.

⑥ Turn *sushi* with right thumb and forefinger, so that the other end can be shaped too. Press sides firmly.

⑦ Repeat as for ⑤.

# 鯵 HORSE MACKEREL

This is horse mackerel. The fish is pink-grey and shiny. When it's fresh, the flesh is almost transparent. The texture is slippery and easy on the tongue. It melts in the mouth. *Aji* is often eaten with soy sauce containing finely chopped long onion, fresh ginger or crushed garlic. These condiments, together with *sushi* rice, make a *sushi* with a difference.

## How To Prepare

① After soaking in salted water, remove "hard scales" from tail end. Insert knife under pectoral fin at right angles and cut off head.

② Make a slit in belly to anal fin. Remove entrails and wash.

③ Insert knife through back and separate meat along backbone.

④ Two fillets, one with bone.

⑤ Insert knife through the back, work along backbone.

⑥ Remove skeleton.

⑦ Slice off the small bones along belly. When cutting, work knife at the right angles to fish.

⑧ With tweezers, pull out small bones along center line.

⑨ Peel back the end of skin at the head with hands.

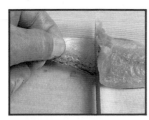

⑩ Pulling the skin with left hand and holding down fish with back of knife, peel off the skin.

⑪ Peel the rest with hand.

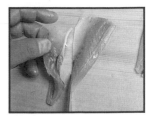

⑫ Cut into halves adjusting to rice ball size. Make some incisions so that it clings to the rice.

## How To Shape *Sushi*

**INGREDIENTS: 2 fingers**

2 slices (about ¹/₂ oz., 15g. each) horse mackerel
About 1²/₅ oz. (40g.) *sushi* rice (See page 94-96)
Ginger root·*Shiso* leaf· Chopped green onion
Lemon slices

① Dip both hands into vinegared water (water:vinegar =3:1). Take some rice (about ²/₃ oz., 20g.) in right fingers and hold gently.

② Take a slice of horse mackerel with left hand, place the rice ball on fish. Press the rice lightly down on fish.

③ Holding sides between thumb and forefinger, roll *sushi* over so that fish is on top.

④ Press sides with right thumb and forefinger.

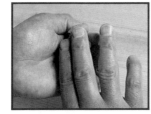

⑤ Shape *sushi* by pressing top with right fingers, and far end with left thumb. Turn *sushi* so that the other end can be shaped too. Check shape again.

⑥ Cut *shiso* leaf into ³/₈ in. (1 cm.) wide strips.

⑦ Place *shiso* strip on *sushi*.

⑧ Place thinly sliced green onion on *shiso*.

⑨ Grate ginger root.

⑩ Place ⑨ on top.

⑪ Garnish with a slice of lemon, if desired.

# SARDINE

The common sardine sliced when fresh and put on *sushi* rice, makes a good tasting mouthful which is also very nutritious. It can be eaten with soy sauce containing fresh ginger or finely chopped long onion. Shiny, slippery and "fishy," the taste of sardine *sushi* is slightly oily. This fish must be eaten shortly after it's been caught, if it's used in *sushi*.

## How To Prepare

① Cut into 2 boneless fillets as for horse mackeral (See page 18, 19). Soak in vinegar about 10 min..

② As sardine skin is soft, it is not necessary to remove it. If desired, skin with hands.

③ Make some incisions so that fish clings to rice ball.

## How To Shape *Sushi*

**INGREDIENTS: 2 fingers**

2 slices (about ¹/₂ oz., 15 g. each) sardine
About 1²/₅ oz. (40 g.) *sushi* rice (See page 94-96)
Dash of *wasabi*

① Dip both hands into vinegared water (water: vinegar = 3:1). Take some rice (about ²/₃ oz., 20 g.) and hold gently. Take a slice of sardine in left hand. With right forefinger, place *wasabi* in center.

② Lay the rice ball on sardine, press down lightly with right forefinger. Holding sides between right thumb and forefinger, roll *sushi* over so that fish is on top.

③ Press sides with right thumb and forefinger.

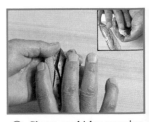

④ Shape *sushi* by pressing top with right fingers, far end with left thumb. Turn *sushi* with right thumb and forefinger, so that the other end can be shaped too. Check shape again.

Sillago can be caught also in South Korea, Africa, Australia. Since the flesh of sillago contains only $1/20$ oz. (1.5 g.) fat among $3 1/2$ oz. (100 g.), the taste is mild and delicate.
Fresh one has bright-gold skin. Usually it's vinegared to use for *sushi*.

## How To Prepare

① Open through back and soak in vinegar as for gizzard shad (See page 16, 17).

② Cut off the tail. Cut the meat into halves.

③ Skin with hands from head to tail.

## How To Shape *Sushi*

**INGREDIENTS: 2 fingers**

2 slices (about $2/3$ oz., 20 g. each) sillago
About $1 2/5$ oz. (40 g.) *sushi* rice (See page 94-96)
Dash of *wasabi*

① Dip both hands into vinegared water (water : vinegar $=3:1$). Take some rice (about $2/3$ oz., 20 g.) and hold gently. Take a slice of sillago in left hand. With right forefinger, place *wasabi* in center.

② Lay the rice ball on fish, press down lightly with right forefinger. This is to make the rice cling to fish.

③ Hold *sushi* between right thumb and forefinger, roll *sushi* over so that fish is on top.

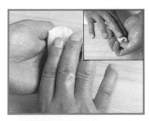

④ Shape *sushi* by pressing top with right fingers, far end with left thumb. Turn *sushi* so that the other end can be shaped too. Check shape again.

21

This is conger eel. *Anago* is pre-cooked—grilled behind the *sushi* bar and then basted with thick *teriyaki* sauce (a sweet sauce made from eel broth, sugar and soy sauce, boiled down over a long period of time). The soft, slightly warm eel, the sweet soy sauce and the vinegared rice together make a particularly "more-ish" *sushi* treat.

## How To Prepare

① Place on board, head to the right. Pin the head down firmly.

② Make deep incision at the base of head. Insert knife through the back as far as backbone, work toward tail.

③ With tip of knife, work through again to open out the whole fillet.

④ Scrape out entrails using knife, and pull out the rest with hands.

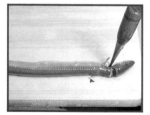

⑤ Cut the bone only at the base of head. Insert knife underneath and work toward tail to remove the bone.

⑥ Cut off dorsal and anal fins.

⑦ Wash thoroughly and drain.

⑧ In saucepan, put 1 cup *dashi* stock, ½ cup soy sauce, ½ cup *mirin*, sprinkle of sugar, bring to boil. Remove scum. Put conger eel, skin side down.

⑨ Cook over high heat with dropped lid or round sheet of foil until boiling. Reduce heat and continue 5 more min..

⑩ Remove the eel from pan immediately and cool.

⑪ Cooked conger eel.

⑫ Cut into about 1 1/8 in. (3 cm.) wide strips.

## How To Shape *Sushi*

**INGREDIENTS: 2 fingers**

2 slices (about 3/8 oz., 12 g. each) conger eel
About 1 2/5 oz. (40 g.) *sushi* rice (See page 94-96)
Thick *teriyaki* sauce

① Dip both hands into vinegard water (water:vinegar =3:1). Take some rice (about 2/3 oz., 20 g.) in right fingers and hold gently.

② Take a slice of conger eel in left hand, place rice ball on and press down lightly with right forefinger. This is to make the rice cling to fish.

③ Holding sides with right thumb and forefinger, turn *sushi* over so that fish is on top.

④ Press sides with right thumb and forefinger.

⑤ Shape *sushi* by pressing with right fingers, and far end with left thumb.

⑥ Turn around and repeat as for ④, ⑤. Check shape again.

⑦ Brush thick *teriyaki* sauce on.

## THICK *TERIYAKI* SAUCE

Thick *teriyaki* sauce is a sauce brushed on cooked conger eel or cuttlefish tentacles to make them tasteful. To make the sauce, professional cooks use the stock in which eels have been boiled.

**[DIRECTONS]**

① Strain the stock through a cloth.
② Bring the stock, sugar, *mirin* and soy sauce to boil.
③ When the scum forms, remove it with a piece of paper towel or tissue.
④ Cook over low heat 5 to 6 hours to about 1/3 quanti-

ty in summer, 1/2 in winter.
⑤ If the sauce "threads" when lifted up with the tip of chopstick, it is thoroughly cooked.

★ In order to keep a certain "viscosity", change thickness of thick *teriyaki* sauce according to the season. Viscosity decreases as the temperature increases. Therefore, in summer the sauce has to be thicker, otherwise it will not stay on the fish.

# 鮑 ABALONE

*AWABI*

Known as abalone or sea snail, this is another favorite with *sushi* eaters. The color ranges from beige-grey to pinkish yellow. Fresh abalone, before it's too rubbery, makes a good contrast in taste and texture when eaten with vinegared rice. As well the addition of *wasabi* and soy sauce gives body to the very subtle flavor of abalone.

## How To Prepare

① Sprinkle with salt to "shrink".

② Hold sharper end. Insert a flat spatula or knife between flesh and shell.

③ Pry off the flesh.

④ Take the flesh out carefully by hand, leaving entrails and filaments still attached to shell.

⑤ Wash and brush with a hard brush.

⑥ Pat dry with cloth.

24

⑦ The part which joins shell and fish is also used, so cut into slices.

⑧ Slice with waving motion.

⑨ Cut the flesh into about ¹/₁₀ in. (3 mm.) slices. Make a few incisions on hard part with tip of knife.

## How To Shape *Sushi*

| INGREDIENTS: 2 fingers |
| --- |

**2 slices (about ¹/₃ oz., 10 g. each) abalone**
**About 1²/₅ oz. (40 g.) *sushi* rice (See page 94-96)**
**Dash of *wasabi***

① Dip both hands into vinegared water (water : vinegar = 3 : 1). Take some rice (about ²/₃ oz., 20 g.) in right fingers and hold gently.

② With left fingers, take a slice of abalone. Place a dab of *wasabi* in center with right forefinger.

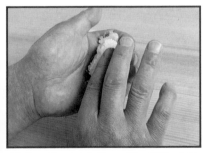

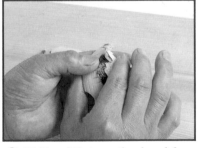

③ Lay the rice ball on fish. With right forefinger, press the rice lightly down on fish.

④ Hold *sushi* between thumb and forefinger, and curl left fingers over to right *sushi* so that fish is on top.

⑤ Press sides with right thumb and forefinger.

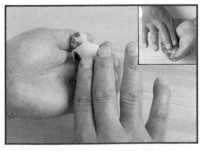

⑥ Shape *sushi* by pressing top with right fingers, and far end with left thumb.

⑦ With right thumb and forefinger, turn *sushi* so that the other end can be shaped too.
Repeat as for ⑤, ⑥. Check shape again.

⑧ Finished.

# 帆立貝 SCALLOP

This is scallop. The part that is eaten is the edible adductor muscle that opens the shell. It's pale beige-yellow in color often with a brown, crusty edging. The taste is delicate, melts in the mouth, and goes well with *sushi* rice.

## How To Prepare

① Hold with hand, flatter side down and hinge on far side. Insert a sharp utensil between shells and pry open.

② Now the shell is open.

③ Insert a sharp utensil between flesh and shell, separate the flesh from shell.

④ Now the shell and flesh are apart.

⑤ Cut off entrails. Pull filaments out pushing finger into hollow where entrails were.

⑥ Separate the adductor muscle from filaments. Sprinkle with salt and wash off sliminess, rubbing the meat gently.

⑦ Now the adductor and filaments are apart.

⑧ If scallop is thick, cut into half thickness.

⑨ Slice to half thickness again, this time leaving the end uncut, so that it can be opened out flat for topping.

## How To Shape *Sushi*

**INGREDIENTS: 2 fingers**

**2 slices (about ¹/₃ oz., 10 g. each) scallop**
**About 1²/₅ oz. (40 g.) *sushi* rice (See page 94-96)**
**2 strips (³/₈ × 4 in., 1 × 10 cm.) *nori* seaweed**
**Dash of *wasabi***

① Dip both hands into vinegared water (water : vinegar = 3 : 1). Take some rice (about ²/₃ oz., 20 g.) in right fingers.

② Take a slice of scallop in left hand, place a dab of *wasabi* in center with right forefinger.

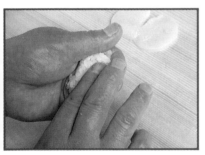

③ Lay the rice on fish and press lightly down with right forefinger. This is to make the rice cling to fish.

④ Holding sides with right thumb and forefinger, turn *sushi* over so that fish is on top.

⑤ Press sides with right thumb and forefinger.

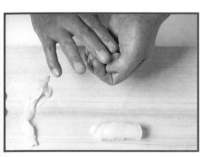

⑥ Shape *sushi* by pressing top with right fingers, and far end with left thumb.

⑦ Turn *sushi* around so that the other end can be shaped too. Repeat as for ⑤, ⑥ Check shape again.

⑧ "Bind" *sushi* with a strip of *nori* seaweed.

This is known as geoduck or horse clam. This is a large hard-shelled clam, yellowish white in color. It has a slightly "shellfish" taste and an elastic type texture. It's best eaten very fresh. The part used in *sushi* is the long muscular siphon which projects out of the shell.

## How To Prepare

① Insert a sharp utensil between the shell halves and pry open.

② Insert a sharp utensil between flesh and shell, pry out the flesh.

③ Wash thoroughly, blanch in boiling water 1 min..

④ Dip in cold water to stop "overcooking."

⑤ Cut off the horny part which sticks out of the shell. This part is used for *sushi* topping.

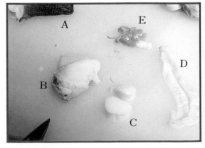

⑥ Divided into parts; A: *Miru* B: *Miru* tongue C: Adductor muscle or joint muscle D: Filaments E: Entrails.

⑦ Remove the black outer skin from *miru*.

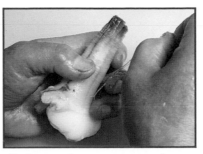

⑧ Remove the transparent membrane.

⑨ Cut open the *miru*.

⑩ Wash and drain.

⑪ Cut off the black hard end.

⑫ Cut diagonally into about 1/3 oz. (10 g.) slices. (Slant knife to the right and slice from the left end, thinly.)

### How To Shape *Sushi*

**INGREDIENTS: 2 fingers**

2 slices (about 1/3 oz., 10 g. each) horse clam
About 1 2/5 oz. (40 g.) *sushi* rice (See page 94-96)
Dash of *wasabi*

① Dip both hands into vinegared water (water:vinegar = 3:1). Take some rice (about 2/3 oz., 20 g.) in right fingers and hold gently.

② Take a slice of horse clam in left hand, and place a dab of *wasabi* in center.

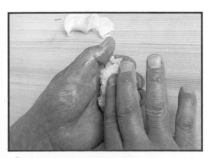

③ Lay the rice ball on fish, press lightly down with right forefinger. This is to make the rice cling to clam.

④ Holding sides between right thumb and forefinger, roll *sushi* over so that fish is on top. Press sides.

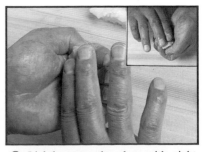

⑤ Lightly press the clam with right fingers, and far end with left thumb. Turn *sushi* so that the other end can be shaped too. Check shape again.

# 赤貝 ARK SHELL

This is ark shell. Softer in texture than the other shell fish, it's pink-orange color makes an attractive topping for a white ball of rice. The taste is delicate and slightly sweet. Often it is decoratively cut by the *sushi* chef. It's difficult to get outside Japan however.

## How To Prepare

① Break part of shell near hinge. Insert a knife and work along edge to separate adductor (part which joins shell and. fish), pry open.

② Work other side of shell and take the flesh out.

③ Flesh and shell are separated.

④ Cut off white parts and hard parts.

⑤ Lift meat, and separate the filament and meat with tip of knife.

⑥ Place the meat down, entrails facing you, slice and open out.

⑦ With a knife, scrape off entrails on both sides.

⑧ Wash quickly in salted water to remove sliminess. Wash under running water.

⑨ Pat dry. Make a few incisions so that fish clings to rice ball.

## How To Shape *Sushi*

**INGREDIENTS: 2 fingers**

**2 ark shells (about 1/3 oz., 10 g. net each)**
**About 1²/₅ oz. (40 g.) *sushi* rice (See page 94-96)**
**Dash of *wasabi***

① Dip both hands into vinegared water (water : vinegar = 3 : 1). Take some rice (about ²/₃ oz., 20 g.) in right fingers, hold gently.

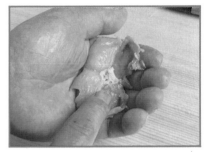

② Take a piece of ark shell in left hand, place a dab of *wasabi* in center with right forefinger.

③ Lay the rice ball on fish and press down lightly with right fingers.

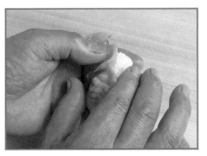

④ Press sides with right forefinger and thumb.

⑤ Holding sides between right thumb and forefinger, roll *sushi* over so that fish is on top.

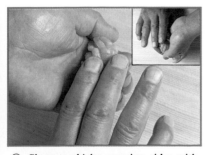

⑥ Shape *sushi* by pressing sides with right forefingers, and far end with left thumb.

⑦ With right thumb and forefinger, turn *sushi* so that the other end can be shaped too.

⑧ Check shape again.

31

This is part of the ark shell, in fact the thread-like edges which connect the flesh to the shell. *Sushi* connoisseurs like it and even casual *sushi* eaters can appreciate the soft texture and mild taste.

## How To Shape *Sushi*

**INGREDIENTS: 2 fingers**

2 ark shell filaments (about $^1/_3$ oz., 10 g. net each)
About $1^2/_5$ oz. (40 g.) *sushi* rice (See page 94-96)
Dash of *wasabi*

## How To Prepare

① Cut off adductor at the base of filament. (See page 30 for preparation.)

② Entwine filaments to form rectangle topping.

③ Entwined filaments.

④ Dip both hands into vinegared water (water:vinegar = 3:1). Take some rice (about $^2/_3$ oz., 20 g.) in right fingers and hold gently. Take filaments in left hand, place a dab of *wasabi* in center.

⑤ Lay the rice ball on fish, press down lightly with right forefinger. This is to make the rice cling to filaments.

⑥ Holding *sushi* between right fingers, curl left fingers over to right *sushi* so that fish is on top. Press sides firmly.

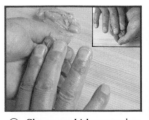

⑦ Shape *sushi* by pressing top with right fingers, far end with left thumb. Turn around to shape the other end. Check shape again.

*Aoyagi* can be found all over Japan. The best season for *aoyagi* is winter-spring in Japan. Besides *sushi*, it is widely used in soups, vinegared dishes, etc. There are two colors; red and white. The red type is good for *sushi*.

## How To Shape *Sushi*

**INGREDIENTS: 2 fingers**

**2 trough shells (about ¹/₃ oz., 10 g. each)**
**About 1²/₅ oz. (40 g.) *sushi* rice (See page 94-96)**
**Dash of *wasabi***

## How To Prepare

① Dip both hands into vinegared water (water:vinegar = 3:1). Take some rice (about ²/₃ oz., 20 g.) in right fingers.

② Take a trough shell in left hand.

③ With right forefinger, place a dab of *wasabi* in center.

④ Lay the rice on fish and press lightly with right forefinger. Holding sides between right fingers, roll *sushi* over so that fish is on top.

⑤ Press sides with right thumb and forefinger.

⑥ Press top with right fingers and far end with left thumb.

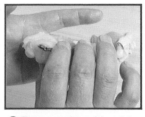

⑦ Turn *sushi* with right thumb and forefinger, so that the other end can be shaped. Repeat as for ⑤, ⑥. Check shape again.

This is Japanese cockle. It is a black and white patterned fish and looks very attractive as *sushi*. It's a small clam shell, difficult to get outside Japan. Since it tastes a bit rubbery if it's frozen, it may be a treat to save for when you visit Japan.

## How To Shape *Sushi*

INGREDIENTS: 2 fingers

2 cockles (about 1/3 oz., 10g. each)
About 1²/₅ oz. (40g.) *sushi* rice (See page 94-96)
Dash of *wasabi*
2 strips *nori* seaweed (³/₈ × 4 in., 1 × 10 cm. each)

① Dip both hands into vinegared water (water : vinegar = 3 : 1). Take some rice (about ²/₃ oz., 20g.) in right fingers and hold gently.

② Take a cockle in left hand, place a dab of *wasabi* in center with right forefinger.

③ Lay the rice ball on fish, and press down lightly with right forefinger. This is to make the rice cling to fish.

④ Holding sides with right thumb and forefinger, roll *sushi* over so that fish is on top. Press sides firmly.

⑤ Shape *sushi* by pressing top with right fingers and far end with left thumb.

⑥ Turn *sushi* around so that the other end can be shaped too. Press sides firmly.

⑦ Repeat as for ⑤ and check shape again.

There are many kinds of octopis, but only a few kinds are edible. Before it's served as *sushi*, boil and slice thinly because, the flesh is tough.
Usually it's pre-boiled and sold at stores. It tends to spoil soon, so choose fresh, elastic flesh.

## How To Prepare

① Remove entrails, eyes and mouth. Cook in generous amount of boiling water, with pinch of salt. (Precooked octopus cut is recommended, as only a few tentacles are needed.)

② Cut into about 1/10 in. (3 mm.) thick slices, waving knife to make ragged surface.

## How To Shape *Sushi*

**INGREDIENTS: 2 fingers**

2 slices octopus tentacles (about 1/3 oz., 10 g. each)
About 1 2/5 oz. (40 g.) *sushi* rice (See page 94-96)
Dash of *wasabi*

① Dip both hands into vinegared water (water : vinegar = 3 : 1). Take some rice (about 2/3 oz., 20 g.) in right fingers and hold gently.

② Take a slice of octopus, and place a dab of *wasabi* in center with right forefinger.

③ Lay the rice ball on fish, press lightly with forefinger.

④ Hold sides between right thumb and forefinger, and roll *sushi* over so that fish is on top. Press sides.

⑤ Lightly press the fish with right fingers, far end with left thumb. Turn *sushi* so that the other end can be shaped too. Check shape again.

# 烏賊 CUTTLEFISH

This is cuttlefish. It comes in all sizes. When it's fresh, it's almost transparent and butter-like, melts in the mouth. The texture is sticky and the taste goes so well with *wasabi* and soy sauce. In color it's smoky white and glistens. Japanese also grill it and eat with ginger soy sauce. Westerners might like to eat it with lemon.

## How To Prepare

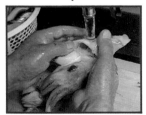

① Wash thoroughly.

② Place on board, tail toward you. Holding with both hands, put thumbs under "body case."

③ Push up the body.

④ Let the cuttlebone slip out toward you.

⑤ Make a slit in body case, on cuttlebone side.

⑥ Hold the tail with left hand, pull tentacles and entrails out.

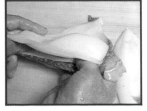

⑦ After washing, peel. (Sprinkle salt on hands for easy handling.) Insert thumbs between skin and meat and carefully separate them.

⑧ Hold the tail and pull the skin off.

⑨ Now the outer skin has been removed.

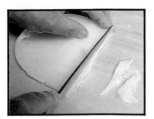

⑩ Cut off tough parts at edges.

⑪ Make very shallow cut at the edge to separate thin membrane.

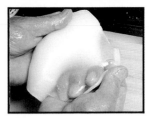

⑫ Remove thin membrane from both sides.

⑬ With a wet cloth, carefully wipe off remaining membrane.

⑭ Check shape.

⑮ Cut into slices, about ⅓ oz. (10g.) each, slanting knife to the right and slice thinly from the left end.

⑯ Make incisions so that fish will cling to rice ball.

## How To Shape *Sushi*

**INGREDIENTS: 2 fingers**

2 slices cuttlefish (about ⅓ oz., 10g. each)
About 1⅖ oz. (40g.) *sushi* rice (See page 94-96)
2 strips *nori* seaweed ⅜ × 4in. 1 × 10cm. each)
Dash of *wasabi*

① Dip both hands into vinegared water (water : vinegar = 3 : 1). Take some rice (about ⅔ oz., 20g.) and hold gently. Take a slice of cuttlefish in left hand. With right forefinger, place *wasabi* in center.

② Lay the rice ball on fish, press down lightly with right forefinger. This is to make the rice cling to fish.

③ Holding sides between right thumb and forefinger, roll *sushi* over so that fish is on top. Press sides.

④ Shape *sushi* by pressing top with right fingers, far end with left thumb.

⑤ With right thumb and forefinger, turn *sushi* so that the other end can be shaped too.

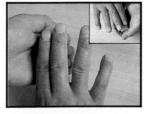

⑥ Press sides again. Repeat as for ④ to shape.

⑦ "Bind" *sushi* with a strip of *nori* seaweed.

These are cuttlefish tentacles. White in color, *geso* is boiled and brushed with thick *teriyaki* sauce before it's put on *sushi* rice. The sweet-salty taste of thick *teriyaki* sauce complements the mild flavor of the boiled cuttlefish. In texture it can be a bit chewy.

## How To Prepare

① After washing well, hold the body tail toward you. Using thumbs, push up body so that cuttlebone slips out.

② Make a slit in body case, on cuttlebone side.

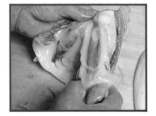

③ Grasp the tail with left hand, pull tentacles and entrails out.

④ Make a slit at the base of tentacles. (Do not break ink bag.)

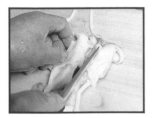

⑤ Remove eyes and mouth.

⑥ Remove entrails.

⑦ Rub with salt to remove sliminess.

⑧ Wash under running water.

⑨ Put tentacles in boiling water and cook.

⑩ Cook until they feel as resilient as bread dough.

⑪ Blanch in cold water.

⑫ Drain.

⑬ Cut off hard part at the base.

⑭ Cut off hard part at the end.

⑮ Cut to top rice balls.

⑯ Make some incisions so that fish clings to rice ball.

## How To Shape *Sushi*

**INGREDIENTS: 2 fingers**

2 slices cuttlefish tentacles (about $1/3$ oz., 10 g. each)
About $1^2/5$ oz. (40 g.) *sushi* rice (See page 94-96)
2 strips *nori* seaweed ($3/8 \times 4$ in., $1 \times 10$ cm. each)
Dash of *wasabi*
Thick *teriyaki* sauce (See page 23)

① Dip both hands into vinegared water (water : vinegar = 3 : 1). Take some rice (about $2/3$ oz., 20 g.) in right fingers, hold gently.

② Take a piece of tentacles in left hand, and place a dab of *wasabi* in center with right forefinger.

③ Lay the rice ball on fish, and press lightly down with right forefinger. Holding sides with right fingers, roll *sushi* over.

④ Press sides. Then, shape *sushi* by pressing top with right fingers, far end with left thumb.

⑤ With right thumb and forefinger, turn sushi and press sides again. Repeat as for ④.

⑥ "Bind" *sushi* with a strip of *nori* seaweed.

⑦ Brush thick *teriyaki* sauce on top.

This kind of shrimp is sometimes called prawn. It's threaded onto bamboo skewers and boiled in slightly salted water before it's shelled and cut open for *sushi*. It's pleasing to the eye with its bright red lines and its tail curling over the end of the ball of rice. A firm favorite with Western *sushi* fans.

## How To Prepare

① Thread with a skewer from belly to head. This is to prevent prawns from curling when boiling.

② Wash skewered prawns clean.

③ In salted boiling water, cook prawns briefly. Take out when one or two start to float.

④ Dip in cold water at once to stop overcooking. Drain and remove skewers.

⑤ Cut off heads.

⑥ Remove shell (from head end to tail).

40

⑦ Remove legs.

⑧ Insert knife into belly, and open out.

⑨ Remove vein along center line using fingers.

## How To Shape *Sushi*

**INGREDIENTS: 2 fingers**

**2 prawns (about ⅓ oz., 10 g. each)**
**About 1²⁄₅ oz. (40 g.) *sushi* rice (See page 94-96)**
**Dash of *wasabi***

① Dip both hands into vinegared water (water : vinegar = 3 : 1). Take some rice (about ⅔ oz., 20 g.) in right fingers and hold gently.

② Take a prawn in left hand, place a dab of *wasabi* in center with right forefinger.

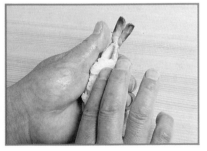

③ Lay the rice ball on prawn, and press down lightly with right forefinger.

④ Holding sides with right thumb and forefinger, turn *sushi* over so that fish is on top.

⑤ Press sides with right fingers.

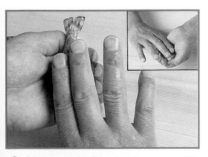

⑥ Shape *sushi* by pressing top with right fingers, far end with left thumb.

⑦ Turn *sushi* around and repeat as for ⑤.

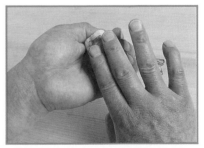

⑧ Repeat as for ⑥. Check shape again.

# 玉子焼 THICK OMELET
*TAMAGOYAKI*

This is Japanese omelet made from chicken eggs and sweetened with sugar. The way it's made is an art; layers of beaten egg, lifted and rolled in a square pan until a square of evenly, just cooked omelet is slid from the pan. It is then cut into pieces and placed on top of *sushi* rice or eaten without rice, like dessert at the end of the meal.

## Directions:

### INGREDIENTS: 1 roll

8 eggs
$1/2$ cup *dashi* stock
$3^1/2$ oz. (100 g.) sugar
1 Tbsp. *mirin*
2 Tbsps. soy sauce
Pinch of salt
Monosodium glutamate
Oil for greasing pan

[Size: $3 \times 6$ in. ($8 \times 15$ cm.), $1^1/8$ in. (3 cm.) thick]

① Into a mixing bowl, crack the eggs. Mix all seasoning ingredients together and add to the bowl. Stir gently with a beater. Do not "beat".

② Grease pre-heated square omelet pan with oil. Use cloth or cotton wool dipped in oil.

③ When the oil gets hot, pour half ladleful egg mixture in, spread from corner to corner tilting the pan over medium heat.

④ When surface hardens fold far $1/3$ over towards you. Fold over again to make 3-layered omelet rectangle. Use chopsticks (at sides of pan).

⑤ Rub the surface of the pan with oiled cloth.

⑥ Slide the omelet to the far end, grease the near end too.

⑦ Pour $1/3$ of remaining mixture in. Lift the roll and mixture underneath.

42

⑧ When the egg is set, roll the omelet toward you twice.

⑨ Rub the surface of the pan with oiled cloth.

⑩ Slide the omelet toward you, grease the far end.

⑪ Pour remaining mixture in. Lift the omelet and let some mixture go underneath.

⑫ When the egg is set, roll the omelet toward you twice. Repeat the process from ⑨ using remaining mixture.

⑬ Slide the cooked omelet on the pan to make a shiny surface.

⑭ Take out from pan. With board or the blade of a knife, press the sides to shape.

⑮ Cut into about 3/8 in. (1 cm.) thick slices.

## How To Shape *Sushi*

**INGREDIENTS: 2 fingers**

2 slices omelet
About 1²/₅ oz. (40 g.) *sushi* rice (See page 94-96)
2 strips *nori* seaweed (³/₈ × 4 in., 1 × 10 cm. each)

① Dip both hands into vinegared water (water : vinegar = 3 : 1). Take some rice (about ²/₃ oz., 20 g.) in right fingers, hold gently.

② Take a slice of omelet in left hand, place the rice ball on. Press down rice lightly with right forefinger.

③ Hold sides with right forefinger and thumb, roll *sushi* over so that omelet is on top.

④ Press sides with right thumb and forefinger.

⑤ Shape *sushi* by pressing top with right fingers, far end with left thumb.

⑥ With right thumb and forefinger, turn *sushi* so that the other end can be shaped too.

⑦ "Bind" *sushi* with a strip of *nori* seaweed.

# 数の子 HERRING ROE

*EDOMAE-ZUSHI*

This is herring roe and an expensive delicacy in Japan. It's suitably known as "yellow diamonds" — yellow in color and as costly as diamonds. In Japan it's eaten on special occasions and "revered" by *sushi* gourmets. For others who can get hold of it, it may be an acquired taste.

## How To Shape *Sushi*

**INGREDIENTS: 2 fingers**

2 pieces herring roe (about ¹/₂ oz., 15g. each) soaked in water to remove excess salt
About 1²/₅ oz. (40g.) *sushi* rice (See page 94-96)
2 strips *nori* seaweed (³/₈ × 4 in., 1 × 10cm. each)
Dash of *wasabi*

① Dip both hands into vinegared water (water:vinegar =3:1). Take some rice (about ²/₃ oz., 20g.) and hold gently. Take a piece of herring roe in left hand. With right forefinger place *wasabi* in center.

② Lay the rice ball on, press down lightly with right forefinger. This is to make the rice cling to fish.

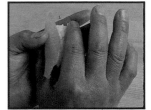

③ Holding sides between right thumb and forefinger, roll *sushi* over so that fish is on top.

④ Press sides with right thumb and forefinger.

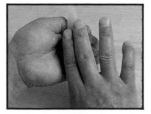

⑤ Shape *sushi* by pressing top with right fingers, far end with left thumb.

⑥ Turn *sushi* with right thumb and forefinger, so that the other end can be shaped too.

⑦ "Bind" *sushi* with a strip of *nori* seaweed.

44

# イクラ SALMON ROE

*Ikura* is salmon roe. The origin of the name *ikura* comes from the Russian word ikra. Russian people got the idea in the process of making caviar from sturgeon. *Ikura* is appealing to the eye with its bright red color it's appetizing. It is rather new as an ingredient for *sushi*, but now it is a *sushi* must.

## How To Shape *Sushi*

**INGREDIENTS:** 2 fingers

About ²/₃ oz. (20g.) red salmon roe
About 1²/₅ oz. (40g.) *sushi* rice (See page 94-96)
2 strips *nori* seaweed (1×7in., 2.5×18cm. each)

① Dip both hands into vinegared water (water:vinegar =3:1). Take some rice (about ²/₃ oz., 20g.) in right fingers and hold gently.

② Press sides between right forefinger and thumb.

③ With right fingers, press the rice down lightly. (Form a lower mound than regular *nigiri-zushi*.)

④ Holding with right thumb and forefinger, roll *sushi* over.

⑤ Repeat as for ②, ③. Check shape again.

⑥ "Bind" *sushi* with a strip of *nori* seaweed.

⑦ With a spoon, place salmon roe on top.

Sea urchin roe is another prized delicacy and for those trying *sushi* for the first time. The oily, rich texture will either delight or dismay. It's a mustard, paste-like topping held in place by a band of *nori* seaweed. The rich taste and texture is quite different to other *sushi* toppings.

### How To Shape *Sushi*

**INGREDIENTS: 2 fingers**

About ²/₃ oz. (20g.) sea ur- chin
About 1²/₅ oz. (40g.) *sushi* rice (See page 94-96)
2 strips *nori* seaweed (1×7 in., 2.5×18 cm. each)
Dash of *wasabi*

① Dip both hands into vin- egared water (water:vinegar =3:1). Take some rice (about ²/₃ oz., 20g.) in right fingers and hold gently.

② Press sides between right forefinger and thumb.

③ With right fingers, press the rice down lightly. (Form lower mound than regular *nigiri-zushi.)*

④ Holding with right thumb and forefinger, roll *sushi* over.

⑤ Repeat as for ②, ③. Check shape again.

⑥ "Bind" *sushi* with a strip of *nori* seaweed. Spread *wasabi* over rice.

⑦ With a spoon, place sea urchin on top.

*Kobashira* is the edible adductor muscle, that opens the shell of *aoyagi*. This *kobashira* is much more expensive than the flesh of *aoyagi*. Before serving, wash lightly in salted water.

## How To Shape *Sushi*

**INGREDIENTS: 2 fingers**

About ²/₃ oz. (20 g.) trough shell scallops
About 1²/₅ oz. (40 g.) *sushi* rice (See page 94-96)
Dash of *wasabi*

① Dip both hands into vinegared water (water:vinegar =3:1). Take some rice (about ²/₃ oz., 20 g.) in right fingers and hold gently.

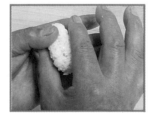

② Press sides between right forefinger and thumb.

③ With right fingers, press the rice down lightly. (Form a lower mound than regular *nigiri-zushi*.)

④ Holding with right thumb and forefinger, turn *sushi*.

⑤ Repeat as for ②, ③. Check shape again.

⑥ "Bind" *sushi* with a strip of *nori* seaweed. Spread *wasabi* over rice.

⑦ Place small scallops on top.

# CHIRASHI-ZUSHI

This is *sushi* rice onto which various ingredients have been scattered (*chirashi*). These ingredients consist of cooked and uncooked shellfish, fish and vegetables. A common combination is tuna, yellowtail, conger eel, omelet, cucumber, grilled squid, shrimp, bamboo shoot, and *shiitake* mushroom. This delicious *sushi* variation is served in a lacquer bowl.

## Directions:

### INGREDIENTS: 1 serving

5¼ oz. (150g.) *sushi* rice
(See page 94-96)
3 slices fatter tuna
3 slices gizzard shad
1 slice yelow jack
2 arkshells
7 julienne strips cuttlefish
1 slice *kamaboko* (steamed fish cake)
Thinly sliced Japanese cucumber
Cooked vegetables
*Oboro* (fish flakes)
Shredded *nori* seaweed
Dash of *wasabi*
Vinegar-pickled ginger slices

① Place *sushi* rice in individual serving bowls. Scatter some shredded *nori* seaweed on rice.

② Lay thick omelet, steamed fish cake, yellow jack and tuna slices on top.

③ Add gizzard shad and squid.

④ Add ark shell.

⑤ Arrange cooked vegetables on top. Fill the space with *oboro* (fish flakes).

⑥ Slide open cucumber slices in your hand to make a fan shape. Garnish with pickled ginger slices and *wasabi*.

48

# PARTY *SUSHI*

# PRESSED SMOKED SALMON *SUSHI*

Popular smoked salmon and lemon slices make an enchanting dish. Serve this splendid dish at a cold buffet.

**[ARRANGEMENT]**

4 cups *sushi* rice (See page 94~96).
1 lb. (450 g.) smoked salmon
2 large sized (8$^1/_8$ × 7 in., 21 × 18 cm.) *temaki katsuo* sheets (dried shaved bonito)
1 Japanese cucumber
1 lemon
2 Tbsp. capers
2 Tbsps. toasted white sesame seeds

NOTE: The following can be substituted for salmon:
1 lb. (450 g.) fresh salmon fillet
To use : Soak in brine. Wipe off water. Marinate in 3 Tbsps. rice vinegar, 2 Tbsps. sugar and $^1/_2$ tsp. salt for 30 min. or longer.

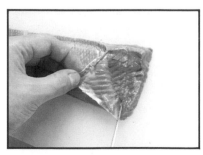

① Cut salmon in half lengthwise, trim off skin.

② Slice salmon diagonally (at 30° angle) into $^1/_4$ in. (7 mm.) thicknesses.

③ Thinly slice lemon. Slice cucumber as illustrated.

④ Grease pyrex dish with oil.

⑤ Lay lemon slices on bottom of dish.

⑥ Put 1 layer of salmon on lemon.

⑦ Add half of *sushi* rice and smooth out, using wet spoon.

⑧ Place *temaki katsuo* sheets on rice.

⑨ Arrange cucumber slices on top and sprinkle with sesame seeds.

⑩ Cover with remainder of rice and smooth out.

⑪ Cover with plastic wrap.

⑫ Place a board on top and apply a weight. Refrigerate for 20 min.

⑬ Remove weight, board, wrap and place plate or tray on top.

⑭ Up-end to unmold.

⑮ Rinse capers and sprinkle on top.

# *SUSHI* WRAPPED IN OMELET

This colorful dish wrapped in thin omelet is ideal for lunch or a light supper, accompanied by soup.

[ARRANGEMENT]

## INGREDIENTS: makes 10

3 cups *sushi* rice (See page 94～96)
10 sheets thin omelet (See page 55)
7 oz. (200 g.) lean ground meat
1/2 cup peas, cooked
1/2 onion
  ⎡ 2/3 tsp. salt
  | 1/8 tsp. pepper
  | 1/2 tsp. light soy sauce
  ⎣ 1/2 tsp. cornstarch
1 Tbsp. toasted sesame seeds
Medium sized (4 × 7 in., 10.5 × 18 cm.) *temaki katsuo* sheet (dried shaved bonito)
Green pepper
Spinach

① Chop onion finely.

② Saute in 1 Tbsp. butter or margarine until light brown.

③ Add ground meat and cook until done.

④ Season with salt, pepper, light soy sauce. Add cornstarch and stir well. Allow to cool.

⑤ Mix cooked peas, toasted sesame seeds and rice.

⑥ Add cooked meat.

⑦ Fill ice cream scoop with mixture (can use wooden spoon).

⑧ Put in center of thin omelet.

⑨ Bring up edges.

⑩ Tie up with strings of cooked spinach. Round, thin slices of green pepper may also be used.

⑪ Fold in half.

⑫ Fold left side over.

⑬ Fold right side over.

⑭ Roll over.

⑮ Decorate with thinly sliced *temaki katsuo* sheet.

# LAYERED *SUSHI*

**All-time favorite ingredients make an artfully composed party dish. Make it at home following our easy recipes for a delicious meat-and-cheese filling.**

[ARRANGEMENT]

**INGREDIENTS: 5-6 servings**

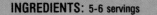

3½ cups *sushi* rice (See page 92 ~ 94)
2 sheets thin omelet (See page 55)
1 lb. (450 g.) lean ground meat
½ onion
⌈ 1 Tbsp. oil
│ 1¼ tsps. salt
│ ¼ tsp. pepper
│ 1 tsp. soy sauce
⌊ 1 tsp. cornstarch
1 Tbsp. white, toasted sesame seeds
¼ cup peas, cooked
1 Japanese cucumber
3 slices cheese
1 Tbsp. finely chopped lemon peel
Some mayonnaise
Dash of paprika

[Size: 7 in. (18 cm.) in diameter, 1¼ in. (5.5 cm.) high *sushi*]

① Cut 2 sheets thin omelet to fit bottom of cake pan (7 in., 18 cm. in diameter). Slice left-over egg thinly.

② Mix left-over egg, lemon peel (finely chopped) and sesame seeds with *sushi* rice.

③ Place 1 thin omelet on bottom of pan.

④ Spread with half of cooked ground meat (See page 52·53).

⑤ Sprinkle over half of cooked peas and cover with half portion of rice mixture. Flatten surface.

⑥ Add cheese slices.

⑦ Cover with other half of ground meat and sprinkle with remainder of peas.

⑧ Spread other thin omelet on top.

⑨ Cover with rest of rice. Press firmly making surface smooth. Cover with plastic wrap and refrigerate for 30 min.

⑩ Remove wrap. Place plate over *sushi*.

⑪ Turn over to unmold *sushi*.

⑫ Slice cucumber diagonally and arrange as illustrated. Add some mayonnaise and paprika, if desired.

## HOW TO MAKE THIN OMELET SHEETS

### INGREDIENTS

[makes 10-12 sheets]
**8 large eggs**
**2²/₃ Tbsps. cornstarch**
**2²/₃ Tbsps. water**
**2 tsps. salt**
**Oil for frying**
[makes 1-2 sheets]
**2 large eggs**
**1 tsp. cornstarch**
**1 tsp. water**
**Pinch of salt**

[size: 9 in. (23 cm.) in diameter]

① Mix cornstarch, water and salt. Add to beaten eggs.

② Grease teflon coated skillet, 9¹/₂ in. (24 cm.) in diameter over medium-low heat. Wipe off excess oil.

③ Pour in just enough beaten egg to cover bottom of skillet.

④ Rotate skillet.

⑤ It's ready when edges curl up and surface becomes glossy.

⑥ Slide out onto waxed paper or plastic wrap. The omelet should be tissue thin. Place paper between each omelet.

# CHIRASHI-ZUSHI (I) VEGETABLE *SUSHI*

The word *chirashi* means "scattered" in Japanese.

A delicately flavored *sushi* rice with an assortment of vegetables in delightful colors.

**INGREDIENTS: 4 servings**

3½ cups *sushi* rice (See page 94~96)
2 dried *shiitake* mushrooms
1½ oz. (40 g.) carrots

A
- ¼ cup *dashi* stock
- ¼ cup *shiitake* soaking water
- 2 Tbsps. *mirin*
- 1½ Tbsps. soy sauce
- 1 Tbsp. *sake*

2 freeze dried *tofu* cakes

B
- 1 cup *dashi* stock
- 3 Tbsp. sugar
- ½ Tbsp. *mirin*
- ½ Tbsp. light soy sauce
- Pinch of salt

1¾ oz. (50 g.) lotus root
- 2 Tbsps. sugar

C
- 3 Tbsps. rice vinegar
- ½ tsp. salt
- 1 tsp. alum

4⅕ oz. (120 g.) seasoned, canned bamboo shoots
⅔ oz. (20 g.) or ½ cup cooked snow peas
¼ cup raisins
2 hard boiled eggs

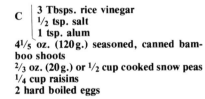

① Soak *shiitake* mushrooms in lukewarm water until soft (30 min.).

② Put liquid aside.

③ Trim off stems and slice thinly.

④ Peel carrot. Make 2 in. (5 cm.) matchsticks.

⑤ Mix ingredients **A**. Cook carrot in it. Add *shiitake* mushrooms and continue to cook until done.

⑥ Soak *tofu* in lukewarm water for 2~3 min. until soft. Squeze out excess water.

⑦ Mix ingredients **B** in saucepan. Heat until sugar dissolves. Add *tofu* cakes. Cook over low heat until juice has been absorbed by *tofu*, about 25 min.

⑧ Set aside to cool.

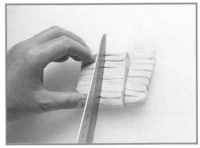

⑨ Cut *tofu* into eighths lengthwise and thirds crosswise.

⑩ Peel lotus, slice into thin round pieces.

⑪ Soak lotus in alum (or vinegar) and water solution (2 cups).

⑫ Cook lotus root in **C** for 4~5 min.

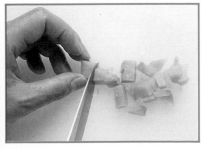

⑬ Dice bamboo shoot into ½ in. (1.5 cm.) cubes.

⑭ Mix carrot, *shiitake* mushrooms, *tofu,* lotus root, bamboo shoot and *sushi* rice.

⑮ Slice cooked snow peas. Add raisins, snow peas, hard boiled egg for decoration.

# CHIRASHI-ZUSHI (II) SEAFOOD *SUSHI*

This *sushi* rice artfully garnished with seafoods is especially suited to summer entertaining. Any firm white fish or shell fish may be used.

| INGREDIENTS: 4 servings |
|---|

4 cups *sushi* rice (See page 94 ~ 96)
1 Japanese cucumber

**A**
  1 Tbsp. rice vinegar
  ¹/₂ Tbsp. sugar
  Pinch of salt

4 prawns
1 squid
1 can crab meat (6 oz., 170 g.)
1 omelet
1 cake steamed fish cake (on wooden board)
2 dried *shiitake* mushrooms

**B**
  ¹/₄ cup *shiitake* soaking water
  1¹/₂ Tbsps. sugar
  1¹/₂ Tbsps. soy sauce
  1 Tbsp. *sake*

¹/₂ sheet *nori* seaweed
1 sheet thin omelet (See page 55)

① Drain crab meat. Remove cartilage. Slice cucumber thinly. Sprinkle with salt and squeeze out water. Marinate in **A**.

② Cook prawns for 4-5 min. (See page 40·41). Remove tail and cut length wise.

③ Insert knife between board and pressed fish. Slice off 6 pieces (¹/₄ in., 7 mm. thick).

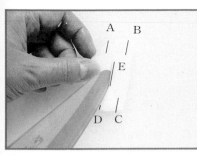

④ Insert ends A, B, C, D into E. Make 4 pieces of steamed fish cake as shown.

⑤ See picture above.

⑥ Slice off 2 more pieces from cake. Dice into ¼ in. (7 mm.) cubes.

⑦ Cook squid in boiling water for 1 min. until skin turns pink.

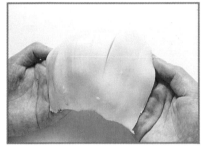

⑧ Make slits as shown, 1¾ in. (2 cm.) apart.

⑨ Place half _nori_ seaweed on top.

⑩ Roll up. Remove excess meat.

⑪ Slice ¼ in. (7 mm.) thick. Soak _shiitake_ mushrooms in water until soft.

⑫ Trim stems off mushrooms. Slice thinly (See page 34·35). Cook in **B** for 4~5 min.

⑬ Squeeze out marinade from cucumbers. Mix _sushi_ rice with crab meat, cucumber, chopped fish cake, and _shiitake_ mushrooms.

⑭ Slice omelet thin.

⑮ Put rice mixture into a bowl, sprinkle with ⑭ . Decorate with squid and prawns.

Old fashioned scattered *sushi* turned into a modern version with chicken *Teriyaki*.

| INGREDIENTS: 4-6 servings |
|---|

3½ cups *sushi* rice (See page 94 ~ 96)
1½ oz. (40g.) carrot
⅓ cup cooked peas
2 dried *shiitake* mushrooms

A
⎰ ¼ cup *dashi* stock
⎱ ¼ cup *shiitake* soaking water
  2 Tbsps. *mirin*
  1½ Tbsps. soy sauce
  1 Tbsp. *sake*

1¾ oz. (50g.) lotus root

B
⎰ 2 Tbsps. sugar
⎱ 3 Tbsps. rice vinegar
  ½ tsp. salt
  1 tsp. alum

7 oz. (200g.) chicken breast, skinned with bones removed
1½ Tbsps. *teriyaki* sauce (See page 61)
4 large eggs

C
⎰ ¼ cup milk
⎱ ⅔ tsp. salt
  Dash of pepper

① Peel carrot and cut into 1 in. (2.5 cm.) long matchsticks. Soak *shiitake* mushrooms until soft. Trim off stems and slice thinly. Cook carrots in **A** and add *shiitake* mushrooms (See page 56·57).

② Peel lotus root, slice into ⅛ in. (5 mm.) thick rounds. Soak in alum (or vinegar) and water solution. In a saucepan mix **B.** When boiling add lotus slices. Cook for 10 min. over low heat.

③ Marinate chicken in *teriyake* sauce for 1 hour.

④ Grill or broil chicken.

⑤ Cut chicken into cubes.

⑥ To make scrambled eggs : break 4 eggs into a bowl, and add **C**. Beat well.

⑦ Melt 1 Tbsp. butter or magarine in skillet and pour in scrambled eggs. Scramble with spatula.

⑧ Mix ① , ② , ⑤ and 2 Tbsps peas, with *sushi* rice.

⑨ Put ¼ of rice mixture into heart-shaped mold. Decorate with peas and scrambled egg.

## HOW TO MAKE *TERIYAKI* SAUCE

### INGREDIENTS: ¼ cup

For 1 lb. (450 g.) of meat
**4 Tbsps. soy sauce**
**1 Tbsp. *mirin***
**1 clove garlic, crushed**
**2 tsps. ginger root, chopped**
**1 tsp. salt**

☆ *Teriyaki* sauce will keep for 1 week in refrigerator.

① Pour soy sauce into a bowl.

② Add *mirin*.

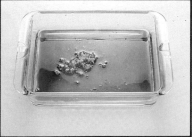

③ Add chopped ginger root.

④ Add crushed garlic (use garlic press).

61

# INARI-ZUSHI

A Japanese version of stuffed *aburage* is a favorite dish with everyone. The *aburage* can be seasoned in advance and frozen for later use. Garnish with shredded red-colored ginger root.

[ARRANGEMENT]

**INGREDIENTS: makes 20**

4½ cups *sushi* rice (See page 94~96)
10 *aburage* (deep-fried *tofu* pouches)

A ⎡ ⅔ cup *dashi* stock
⎢ 5 Tbsps. sugar
⎣ 4 Tbsps. soy sauce

⅔ oz. (20 g.) *kampyo* (dried gourd strips)

B ⎡ ¼ cup *dashi* stock
⎢ 3 Tbsps. sugar
⎣ 3 Tbsps. soy sauce

4 medium sized dried *shiitake* mushrooms
1 cup diced carrots

C ⎡ ⅓ cup *dashi* stock
⎢ ⅓ cup *shiitake* soaking water
⎢ 2 Tbsps. *mirin*
⎣ 1½ Tbsps. soy sauce

⎣ 1 Tbsp. *sake*
1 Japanese cucumber
Salt

① Press *aburage* with rolling pin for easy opening.

② Cut 7 pieces in half.

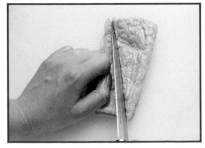

③ Cut 2 pieces into triangles.

④ Trim 3 edges of remaining piece.

⑤ With thumb as illustrated, open *aburage*.

⑥ In a large saucepan, boil 3 cups of water. Put in *aburage* and cook for 2 min. to remove excess grease. Drain well.

⑦ In a saucepan, heat ingredients **A**. Add *aburage*. Cook over medium heat for about 20 min. or until most of the liquid has been absorbed. Allow to cool or put in refrigerator.

⑧ Soak *kampyo* (gourd strips) in water until soft.

⑨ Wash in salted water (1 Tbsp. salt). Rinse well.

⑩ In medium size saucepan, put 2½ cups cold water. Add *kampyo* (gourd strips). Cook 15 min. Drain.

⑪ In a saucepan boil **B**. Add ⑩. Cook over medium heat 20 min. Cool.

⑫ Chop into ¼ in. (7 mm.) squares. Set aside.

⑬ Soften *shiitake* mushrooms. Trim stems. Cut into ¼ in. (7 mm.) cubes.

⑭ Peel carrot, chop finely. Cook mushrooms and carrots in **C**.

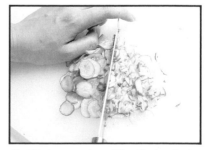

⑮ Wash cucumber. Slice finely. Soak in salted water (1 Tbsp. salt) for 5 min.. Drain and squeeze well. Set aside.

# INARI-ZUSHI

⑯ Mix cooked vegetables with rice. Add cucumber. Mix well.

⑰ Using a spoon fill *aburage* pouches.

⑱ Close.

⑲ Fill triangular bags.

⑳ Fold as shown.

㉑ Take final *aburage* piece and on bamboo mat open out, wrong side up. Spread with rice (¼ in., 7mm. thick), leaving ⅜ in. (1cm.) at front and ¾ in. (2cm.) at end uncovered.

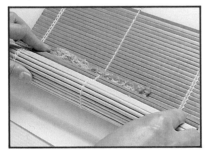

㉒ Roll.

㉓ Push in ends.

㉔ Cut into 3 pieces.

## INARI-ZUSHI

The fox appears in many guises in Japanese folklore. A most mischievous animal, it often plays tricks on humans. The fox is also, the messenger of the god of the harvest, *Inari*.

As one of the fox's favorite foods is *aburage*, *sushi* made with *aburage* is called *Inari-zushi*.

Many ingredients are added to *sushi* rice that is then stuffed into cooked pouches made of *aburage*.

*Aburage* is found in cans or plastic bags in the refrigerator case, 3 to 5 pieces per pack. To remove excess oil, pour boiling water over sheets, drain briefly, and press in paper towels.

## JAPANESE CUCUMBER

The Japanese cucumber is about 8-8½ in. (20-21.5cm.) in length and about half the thickness of the American cucumber. It is tender and crisp in texture and flavorful. The skin is thinner and more tender than the American cucumber. It is not necessary to peel the skin off. The recipes here throughout this book use the Japanese cucumber. Look for a Japanese cucumber that is firm and uniform in color. It is available at most oriental groceries. If unavailable, find the youngest cucumbers you can find and peel the skin and remove seeds. English cucumbers and zucchini can be substituted for Japanese cucumbers.

## ★ QUICK AND EASY

**INGREDIENTS:** makes 20

4½ cups  cooked  rice (See page 94~96)
20 bags cooked  *aburage*
*Sushi-no-moto* powder
Cooked *sushi* vegetables
Chopped parsley

① In large *sushi* bowl mix hot rice with instant *sushi-no-moto* powder.

② Add cooked vegetables and mix well.

③ Add chopped parsley if desired.

④ Fill ready made seasoned *aburage* bags with rice mixture.

## Quick & Easy method

• You can buy the vinegar mixture (in powder or liquid), the cooked vegetables (in cans or bottles), and the cooked *aburage* (in cans or vacuum packages). All you have to do is mix with cooked rice. It takes only a few minutes.

You can easily make a satisfying dish for unexpected guests. It is also good for late suppers. It is quite filling and not fattening. Add chopped parsley, ham, meat, etc. and make your own *inari-zushi*. Thurn the *aburage* inside-out and push the stuffing in.

Try and create your own special *inari-zushi*.

# LOG SHAPED *SUSHI*

A fresh fish in season marinated in sweet-and-sour sauce will be prized among your guests. Serve as a light main dish accompanied by your favorite salad or soup.

[ARRANGEMENT]

**INGREDIENTS: 3-4 servings**

3 cups *sushi* rice (See page 94~96)
7 oz. (200 g.) striped bass fillet or summer flounder
A ⎱ 3 Tbsps. rice vinegar
   ⎰ 1 Tbsp. *mirin*
¹⁄₆ oz. (5 g.) ginger root
1 lemon
2 Tbsps. toasted white sesame seeds
1 large sized (8¹⁄₈ × 7 in., 21 × 8 cm.) *temaki katsuo* sheets (dried shaved bonito)
A little *wasabi*

① Sprinkle salt on fish. Wipe off with paper towel. Marinate in **A** for 1 hour.

② Wipe dressing off fish and trim so entire piece is same thickness.

③ Peel ginger root.

66

④ Slice into match stick size pieces.

⑤ Soak in water.

⑥ Chop lemon peel.

⑦ Mix toasted white sesame seeds into rice.

⑧ Add lemon peel, mix well.

⑨ Dab *wasabi* along center of fish.

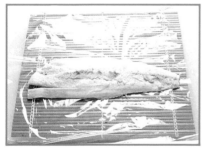

⑩ Place a sheet of plastic wrap on bamboo mat and put fish fillet on top.

⑪ Drain ginger root and put down center of fillet.

⑫ Cut *temaki katsuo* sheet into bite-size and place on top of fish.

⑬ Shape *sushi* rice: like log as shown and place on top of fish.

⑭ Roll up.

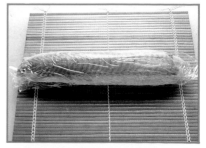

⑮ Leave in wrap for 1 hour in the refrigerator. Slice into serving rounds.

# TAZUNA-ZUSHI CANDY CANE *SUSHI*

This is a colorful assortment of food arranged like a candy-cane. It can be served as an appetizer or as a main course.

[ARRANGEMENT]

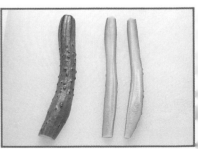

| INGREDIENTS: 4-6 servings | |
|---|---|

4 cups *sushi* rice (See page 99～96)
3 cooked prawns (See page 40·41)
2 oz., (60 g.) pickled gizzard shad
1 Japanese cucumber
1 sheet thin omelet (See page 55)
1/4 sheet *nori* seaweed

① Cut in half lengthwise. Trim off tail.

② Cut pickled gizzard shad halves, same length as prawn.

③ Cut cucumber in half lengthwise, cut lengths, lengthwise in half again.

④ Cut cucumber lengths into 3, or the same size as prawn. Then cut into julienne strips.

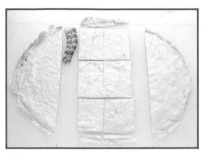

⑤ Cut thin omelet into 4 lengthwise. Then cut 2 lines in center into 3 horizontally.

⑥ Slice both side ends of omelet into ½ in. (1.5 cm.) wide pieces.

⑦ On plastic wrap, arrange ingredients at 30° angle as shown. Place *nori* seaweed on top.

⑧ Add rice.

⑨ Indent center using fingers.

⑩ Put cucumber sticks in indentation.

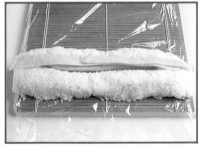

⑪ Place thin omelet on top.

⑫ Begin rolling.

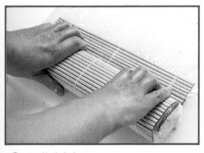

⑬ Roll tightly.

⑭ Leave for 30 min. with wrap on. It is easily sliced with wrap still on.

## TIP

The color counts just as much as the taste. For a better result:
① Make an attractive pattern. Imagine the color schem first in your mind. (For example, prawns and tuna would not make attractive patterns)
② Adjust the length and width of the fish pieces.
③ If you are a beginner, lay a wide sheet of *nori* seaweed across the thimmings so that they cling to the rice.

# SMALL ROLL

Once you have mastered the art of making a rolled *sushi*, you can make a variety of forms with the filling of your choice.

[ARRANGEMENT]

## a. *KAMPYO* ROLL

INGREDIENTS: 4 rolls
1 oz. (30 g.) cooked *kampyo* (See page 63)
2 sheets *nori* seaweed
1¹/₂ cup *sushi* rice (See page 94 ~ 96)

① Cut *nori* seaweed in half lengthwise (4×7 in., 10.5×18 cm.) Place *nori* seaweed on mat, shiny side down.

② Put ¹/₄ of *sushi* rice on ① . Spread ¹/₈ in. (5 mm.) thick with the back of a spoon. Leave 1 in. (2.5 cm.) uncovered at both ends.

③ Place cooked *kampyo* in center.

④ Begin rolling by lifting mat and pressing *kampyo* with fingers.

⑤ Roll up tightly. Press ends. One roll makes 6 pieces.

## b. *TEKKA* ROLL

**INGREDIENTS: 4 rolls**
2 oz. (60 g.) tuna
2 sheets *nori* seaweed
1½ cups *sushi* rice (See page 94 ~ 96)
1 Tbsp. *wasabi*

① Cut tuna in pieces same length as *nori* seaweed and ½ in. (1.5 cm.) thick.

② Spread ¼ of rice on *nori* seaweed. Put some *wasabi* in center of rice. Roll up as shown in **a**-roll.

## c. *KAPPA* ROLL

**INGREDIENTS: 4 rolls**
1 Japanese cucumber or ½ zucchini
2 sheets *nori* seaweed
1½ cups *sushi* rice (See page 94 ~ 96)
1 Tbsp. *wasabi*.

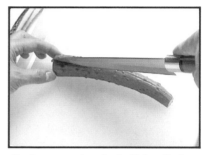

① Cut cucumber into lengths the same size as *nori* seaweed.

② Cut cucumber in half lengthwise. Cut these pieces again lengthwise to make 4 pieces. Roll up, as shown in **a**-roll

## d. *OSHINKO* ROLL

**INGREDIENTS: 4 rolls**
2 oz. (60 g.) pickled *daikon* (gaint radish)
2 sheets *nori* seaweed
1½ cup *sushi* rice (See page 94 ~ 96)

① Cut pickled *daikon* radish lengthwise, same size as *nori* seaweed.

② Cut into ⅜ in. (1 cm.). thick circular lengths. Roll up, as shown in **a**-roll.

## VARIATION: CUTTING METHOD.

**BASIC CUT**
Slice into 6, wetting knife after each cut.

**VARIATION CUT**
Put skewers through 4 rolled *sushi* and then cut into 4 making 16 pieces.

## VARIATION: ROLLING METHOD

**ROLLING**
Roll as for small rolled *sushi* and then press one end together to make triangular shape.

**ARRANGE**
6 pieces of *sushi* to look like petals.

# MEDIUM ROLL

**Colorful fillings rolled in *nori* seaweed, cut into thick slices.**

[ARRANGEMENT]

## a. WHITE MEAT FISH, OMELET AND JAPANESE CUCUMBER ROLL

**INGREDIENTS: 2 rolls**
$3^1/_2$ oz. (100 g.) white fish fillet
2 Tbsps. *teriyaki* sauce (See page. 61)
$1^3/_4$ oz. (50 g.) thick omelet
1 Japanese cucumber
2 sheets *nori* seaweed
$1^1/_2$ cups *sushi* rice (See page 94~96)

① Marinate fish in *teriyaki* sauce for 1 hour.

② Heat oil in skillet, grill fish on both sides. Cut into pieces 2 in. (5 cm.) long, $3/_4$ in. (2 cm.) wide pieces.

③ Cut thick omelet into $1/_4$ in. (7 mm.) pieces

④ Spread half of rice onto *nori* seaweed. Flatten with back of wooden spoon.

⑤ Leave $3/_8$ in. (1 cm.) at front and $3/_4$ in. (2 cm.) at end uncovered.

⑥ Place all ingredients in center.

⑦ Lift bamboo mat with fingers, holding ingredients with fingers.

⑧ Roll tightly.

⑨ Press ends with fingers.

⑩ Cut in half.

⑪ Makes 6-8 pieces.

## b. SPINACH AND SARDINE ROLL

**INGREDIENTS: 2 rolls**
$1/2$ bunch spinach
1 can sardines (2 oz., 60 g.)
2 sheets *nori* seaweed 4, small sized
$(2 \times 3^{1}/_{2}$ in., $5 \times 9$ cm.) *temaki katsuo*
sheets (dried shaved bonito)
$1^{1}/_{2}$ cups *sushi* rice (See page 94 ~ 96)

① Cook spinach in salted water, Drain and squeeze out excess water.

② Spread half *sushi* rice ($1/4$ in., 7 mm. thick) leaving $3/8$ in. (1 cm.) at front and $3/4$ in. (2 cm.) at end uncovered.

③ Place 2 *temaki katsuo* sheets in center.

④ Put spinach and drained sardines on top as shown.

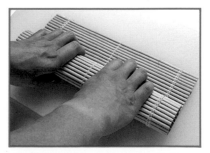

⑤ Lift bamboo mat as shown above. Roll *sushi* using mat, as shown in **a**-roll.

# JUMBO ROLL

a

b

The Japanese use *nori* seaweed in many courses when cooking. The color combination is essential to the success of many Japanese dishes.

## a. WIENER SAUSAGE, JAPANESE CUCUMBER AND CHEESE ROLL

INGREDIENTS: 2 rolls
2 cooked wiener sausages
2¹/₂ oz. (70 g.) cheese of your choice
1 Japanese cucumber
3 sheets *nori* seaweed
2¹/₅ cups *sushi* rice (See page 94 ~ 96)
1 Tbsp. toasted sesame seed and salt mixture

① Cut cucumber in lengths equal in size to shorter sides of *nori* seaweed 7 in. (18 cm.)

② Then cut in half, lengthwise, and then in quarters.

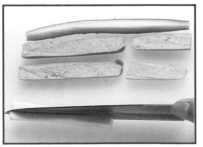

③ Cut wiener sausages in half lengthwise. Cut in half crosswise. Cut cheese.

④ Cut 1 sheet of *nori* seaweed in half.

⑤ Place 1¹/₂ sheets of *nori* seaweed on bamboo mat, shiny side down. Over-lap edges. Spread rice over (¹/₄ in., 7 mm. thick), leaving ³/₈ in. (1 cm.) at front and ³/₄ in. (2 cm.) at end uncovered.

⑥ Arrange sausage, cucumber and cheese as illustrated. Sprinkle with sesame seed and salt mixture.

⑦ Start rolling.

⑧ With bamboo mat roll up.

⑨ Roll tightly.

⑩ Unroll mat and push rice in at both ends.

⑪ Cut in half. Makes 6 pieces. Wet knife before slicing.

## b. HAWAIIAN ROLL

**INGREDIENTS: 2 rolls**
**4 oz. (100 g.) ham**
**2 slices canned pineapple**
**1/2 bunch spinach**
**3 sheets *nori* seaweed**
**2 1/5 cups *sushi* rice (See page 94 ~ 96)**

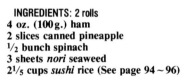

① Cut 1 sheet of *nori* seaweed lengthwise in half. Cook spinach in salted water. Drain off excess water.

② Cut spinach same length as longer side of *nori* seaweed (7 in., 18cm.)

③ Slice ham into 1/4 in. (7mm.) thick rounds.

④ Cut pineapple slices.

⑤ Place ingredients as shown. Roll up *sushi* using mat, as show in **a**-roll. Roll tightly, push rice in at ends. Cut in half. Makes 6 pieces.

# TOMOE-ZUSHI PAIR SUSHI

This variation of rolled *sushi* is ideal for an intimate dinner, served with a tossed green salad and soup.

**[ARRANGEMENT]**

**INGREDIENTS: 6 pairs**

1/2 bunch spinach
1 can tuna (7 oz., 200 g.)
1 Tbsp. mayonnaise
2 sheets *nori* seaweed
1 cup *sushi* rice (See page 94 ~ 96)

① Drain tuna and mix with mayonnaise. Cook spinach. Drain well.

② Spread half of rice on *nori* seaweed leaving 3/8 in. (1 cm.) uncovered in front. Place tuna and spinach on upper 1/3 of rice.

③ Lift bamboo mat and start rolling.

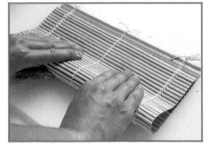

④ Press down toward end of roll.

⑤ Roll in like a pear shape.

⑥ Cut in half.

⑦ Put together as shown.

⑧ Place on bamboo mat. Make rectangular shape. Cut into 3.

## VARIATION

① Sprinkle powdered instant _sushi_ dressing over rice while hot. Mix in, using slicing motion. Use a wooden spatula. Allow to cool.

② Spread rice on $^2/_3$ of _nori_ leaving $^3/_8$ in. (1 cm.) uncovered at front.

③ Place tuna and spinach in center.

④ Start to roll it up. press end of roll.

⑤ Fold unrolled _nori_ toward the roll. Cut into 8 pieces. Wet knife after each slice.

## HOW TO ARRANGE

# GREEN ROLL

Fresh green parsley adds a distinctive flavor and texture. Freshly cut herbs can also be used.

[ARRANGEMENT]

## INGREDIENTS: 2 rolls

1 bunch parsley
1 Japanese cucmber
2 large sized (8$\frac{1}{8}$×7 in., 21×18 cm.) *temaki katsuo* sheets (dried shaved bonito)
1 can salmon (7 oz., 200 g.)
1 Tbsp. toasted sesame seed and salt mixture
1$\frac{1}{2}$ cups *sushi* rice (See page 94~96)

① Wash parsley and chop finely.

② Drain salmon.

③ Remove bones and skin.

78

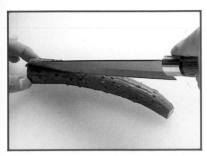

④ Cut cucumber lengthwise into quarters.

⑤ Lay plastic wrap over bamboo mat. Spread rice ¹/₄ in. (7mm.) thick and same size as *temaki katsuo* sheet.

⑥ Place the *temarki katsuo* sheet on rice. Place flaked salmon on top.

⑦ Arrange cucumber as shown.

⑧ Sprinkle sesame seed and salt mixture on top.

⑨ Lift bamboo mat with thumb and index fingers pushing ingredients towards you with fingers.

⑩ Roll up carefully. Remove mat and unwrap plastic.

⑪ Sprinkle chopped parsley around rolled rice.

⑫ Reshape with plastic wrap and bamboo mat if necessary.

---

## PARSLEY

Parsley, which is used extensively as a garnishing, contains a lot of vitamins A and C, iron, calcium, etc. Since it has a strong fragrance it should be used sparingly. Care should be taken in preparing parsley to serve. Minced parsley mixted with meat dishes, salads or soups is well known way to use it. When using minced parsley, first squeeze out all the water with cheese cloth. Don't put parsley wrapped in cheese cloth under the tap. This method of washing it will damage the color and fragrance which are, after all, the special features of the vegetable.

For those who can not eat parsley raw, we suggest frying it. Wash parsley, remove water with a cloth, flour lightly, then fry. If over-fried, it will become limp and fragile. So, cook with care so it will be crisp when removed from the oil.

Parsley is just a small vegetable which is often neglected. Serve it as often as you can.

**PARSLEY**

# THIN OMELET ROLL

a

b

There are many ways to prepare and serve eggs. This is one colorful and easy-to-make dish.

## a. CORNED BEEF AND ASPARAGUS ROLL

INGREDIENTS: 2 rolls
2 sheets thin omelet (See page 55)
$\frac{1}{2}$ can corned beef
2 spears asparagus
2 small pickles
$1\frac{1}{2}$ cups *sushi* rice (See page 94~96)

① Cook asparagus in salted water. put aside.

② Cut pickles lengthwise into quarters.

③ Flake corned beef.

④ Place plastic wrap on bamboo mat. Lay thin omelet sheet on top and spread with rice (as shown). Arrange all ingredients in center of rice.

⑤ To roll up thin omelet press lightly and lift mat with thumbs as shown.

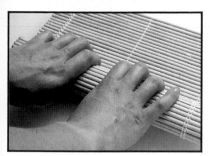

⑥ Roll, pressing firmly.

⑦ Remove mat.

⑧ Cut in half and then into thirds (makes 6 pieces).

## b. BEEF AND *DAIKON* ROLL

**INGREDIENTS: 2 rolls**
2 sheets thin omelet (See page 55) *daikon* (giant radish)
1 Tbsp. toasted white sesame seeds
3½ oz. (100 g.) sirloin steak
2 Tbsps. *teriyaki* sauce (See page 61)
1½ cusp *sushi* rice (See page 94 ~ 96)

① Marinate meat in *teriyaki* sauce for 1 hour or longer.

② Cook meat in skillet, adding a small amount of *teriyaki* sauce.

③ Cook meat well on both sides. Add more sauce if necessary.

④ Slice meat into ¼ in. (7 mm.) thicknesses.

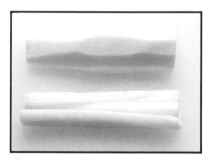

⑤ Cut *daikon* into pieces ½ in. (1.5 cm.) thick and 9½ in. (24 cm.) length.

⑥ Lay plastic wrap on bamboo mat and put on a sheet of thin omelet. Spread rice on top. Arrange meat and *daikon* as illustrated. Sprinkle with sesame seeds.

⑦ Roll up, as shown in **a**-roll,

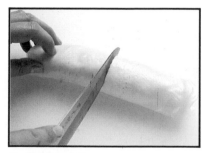

⑧ Cut into 4 pieces.

## *TEMAKI-ZUSHI* (I) *NORI* SEAWEED ROLL

Take away the worry and fuss of cooking. Let your guests make their own *sushi*. It will be refreshing and delightful party dish.

[ARRANGEMENT]

## ☆ HAND-ROLL IN *NORI* SEAWEED

**NORI SEAWEED**

(4 × 7 in., 10.5 × 18 cm.)

**SUSHI RICE**

See page 94 ~ 96

+

### a. *NATTO, SHISO* LEAF AND GREEN ONION ROLL

**INGREDIENTS: 4 rolls**
3½ oz. (100 g.) *natto*
4 *shiso* leaves
2 Tbsps. chopped green onion
A little mustard
A little soy sauce

① Mix *natto* with soy sauce and mustard.

② Cut *nori* seaweed lengthwise in half.

③ Place *nori* seaweed on left palm, add a small amount of rice.

④ Add *shiso, natto* and chopped green onion.

⑤ Wrap *nori* seaweed around it.

⑥ Roll up from left to right.

⑦ It's ready to eat.

## b. SMOKED SALMON AND ONION SLICE ROLL

INGREDIENTS: 4 rolls
1³/₄ oz. (50 g.) smoked salmon
¹/₄ dry onion sliced in thin rounds.
A [ ¹/₄ cup rice vinegar
    1 tsp. salt

① Slice salmon diagonally.

② Marinate sliced onion in **A** for 15 min.

③ Place a little rice on *nori* seaweed, add smoked salmon and sliced onion. Roll up, as shown in **a**-roll.

## c. JAPANESE CUCUMBER AND SESAME SEED ROLL

INGREDIENTS: 4 rolls
1 Japanese cucumber
Some toasted sesame seed and salt mixture.
A little *wasabi*

① Cut cucumber lengthwise in half.

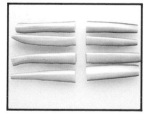

② Continue cutting to make 8 pieces. (lengthwise like matchsticks).

③ Place *nori* seaweed on left palm, add a little rice.

④ Dab a little *wasabi*

⑤ Add cucumber sticks and sprinkle with sesame seeds and salt mixture.

⑥ Roll up from left to right.

## d. AVOCADO, STEAMED FISH CAKE AND JAPANESE CUCUMBER ROLL

**INGREDIENTS: 4 rolls**
**1 avocado**
**1/4 lemon**
**4 sticks steamed fish cake**
**1 Japanese cucumber**

① Peel avocado.

② Cut into wedges and remove seed.

③ Cut into 4, then into 8 pieces.

④ Sprinkle with lemon juice.

⑤ Place *nori* seaweed on left palm. Put on a little rice, avocado and steamed fish cake.

⑥ Add cucumber stick.

⑦ Roll up from left to right.

☆*SUSHI* PARTIES ARE FUN TO TRY AT HOME.
The guests can put together their own *sushi*.
To do this you will need plenty of the following:

*Sushi* rice (See page 94～96)
Crisp sheets of *nori* seaweed
A selection of seafood including tuna, prawns/shrimps, squid, shellfish and any other fish in season.
Smoked salmon, omelet, shiso leaves
Soy sauce
*Wasabi*

Discover the unique texture of the *temaki katsuo* sheet. It is made of traditional Japanese dried bonito flakes. This could be a Japanese style cocktail snack.

[ARRANGEMENT]

## ☆ HAND-ROLL IN *TEMAKI KATSUO* SHEET

**TEMAKI KATSUO SHEET (DRIED SHAVED BONITO)**

Medium size (4 × 7 in., 10.5 × 18 cm.)

*SUSHI* RICE

See page 94 ~ 96

**+**

### a. ASPARAGUS AND CARROT ROLL

INGREDIENTS: 4 rolls
1 carrot
4 spears asparagus
1 Tbsp. toasted sesame seed and salt mixture
1/6 oz. (5 g.) shaved bonito flakes
A little soysauce

① Peel carrot.

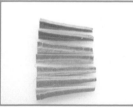

② Cut into 4 in. (10 cm.) long, 3/8 in. (1 cm.) wide pieces.

③ Cook asparagus in salted water. Dip in cold water. Drain well. Cut in half.

④ Season shaved bonito flakes with soy sauce.

⑤ Place *temaki katsuo* sheet in left hand and place a little rice on it.

⑥ Put carrot and asparagus on top.

⑦ Sprinkle with bonito flakes and sesame seed. Roll up from left to right.

## b. JAPANESE CUCUMBER ROLL

**INGREDIENTS: 4 rolls**
**1 Japanese cucumber**
**A littel *wasabi***

① Place *temaki katsuo* sheet on left hand. Put a little rice, *wasabi* and cucumber on top.

② Roll up from left to right.

③ It's ready to eat.

## c. SARDINE AND PARSLEY ROLL

**INGREDIENTS: 4 rolls**
**1 can sardine**
**1/2 bunch parsley**

① Wash parsley. Chop finely.

② Place *temaki katsuo* sheet on left hand. Put on a little *sushi* rice, a sardine and some parsley.

③ Roll up from left to right.

## d. MUSHROOM, *SHISO* LEAF, JAPANESE CUCUMBER AND PICKLED PLUM PASTE ROLL

**INGREDIENTS: 4 rolls**
**4 fresh mushrooms**
**4 *shiso* leaves**
**1 Japanese cucumber**
**2 tsps. pickled plum paste**

① Clean mushrooms. Slice thin.

② Place *temaki katsuo* sheet on left palm. Put rice on top. Add *shiso* leaf and pickled plum paste.

③ Arrange sliced mushrooms on top. Roll up from left to right.

## VARIATIONS

### *TEMAKI KATSUO* SHEET
### (DRIED SHAVED BONITO)

Medium size (4×7in., 10.5×18cm.)

### a. SHRIMP AND JAPANESE CUCUMBER ROLL

**INGREDIENTS: 4 rolls**
**4 cooked prawns/shrimp**
**(See page 40·41)**
**1 Japanese cucumber**
**A little *wasabi***

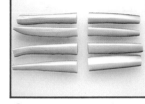

① Cut cucumber into 8 match stick pieces.

② Put together cucumber, shrimp and *wasabi* and roll up in *temaki katsuo* sheets from left to right.

③ It's ready to eat.

### b. SMOKED SALMON, ONION AND AVOCADO ROLL

**INGREDIENTS: 4 rolls**
**1³/₄ oz. (50g.) smoked salmon**
**¹/₄ dry onion sliced into thin rounds**
**A ⎡ ¹/₄ cup rice vinegar**
**⎣ 1 tsp. salt**
**1 avocado**
**2 Tbsps. lemon juice**

① Soak onion in **A** for 15 min. Slice salmon diagonally. Peel avocado and cut into wedges (See page 84). Sprinkle with lemon juice.

② Arrange salmon, avocado, and onion as illustrated.

③ Roll up from left to right.

### c. CAVIAR AND CHOPPED ONION ROLL

**INGREDIENTS: 4 rolls**
**1³/₄ oz. (50g.) caviar**
**¹/₄ cup chopped onion**

① Place ¹/₄ of caviar on *temaki katsuo* sheet as illustrated.

② Put chopped onion on top.

③ Roll up from left to right.

# TEMAKI-ZUSHI (III) THIN OMELET ROLL

**Pleasant for a light luncheon. All-time favorites; eggs, are especially good with *sushi* rice.**

[ARRANGEMENT]

## ☆ HAND-ROLL IN THIN OMELET

**THIN OMELET**

**SUSHI RICE**

**+**

See page 55

See page 94 ~ 96

### a. HAWAIIAN ROLL

**INGREDIENTS: 4 rolls**
2¹/₂ oz. (70g.) ham
2 slices canned pineapple

① Cut pineapple into 8.

② Cut ham into ¹/₄ in. (7mm.) thicknesses.

③ Cut thin omelet in half.

④ Spread *sushi* rice on center of thin omelet as illustrated.

⑤ Place ham and pineapple on top.

⑥ Fold over left side.

⑦ Fold over right side.

## b. WIENER SAUSAGE AND CHEESE ROLL

**INGREDIENTS: 4 rolls**
**2-3 cooked wiener sausages**
**2¹/₂ oz. (70 g.) cheese**

① Cut sausages lengthwise in half. Cut cheese into ¹/₂ in. (1.5 cm.) thick pieces.

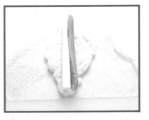

② Cut omelet in half. Place *sushi* rice, sausage, cheese on top.

③ Fold left side towards center and fold right side over the top.

## c. RED LEAF LETTUCE AND SALAMI ROLL

**INGREDIENTS: 4 rolls**
**2 slices salami**
**2 red leaf lettuce leaves**

① Cut salami into ¹/₄ in. (7 mm.) wide pieces.

② Cut omelet in half and place rice on top. Put salami and red leaf lettuce on top.

③ Fold left side towards center and fold right side over the top.

## CHICKEN AND QUAIL EGGS

Chicken eggs are high protein food. The protein value is 100 which is the most ideal value of all foods. The white contains pure protein only, but the yolk has iron and vitamin A as well.

The yolk also contains lecithin which prevents the increase of cholesterol in the blood. Some analysts report, therefore, that the cholesterol content in the chicken egg is relatively high, but cholesterol in the blood does not increase when eggs are eaten. The protein content in a chicken egg is about ¹/₆ oz. (5g.) in weight, which is roughly equivalent to that contained in 180 cc. of cow's milk. However, it is a representative acid-forming food, therefore, you must eat vegetables and/or fruits when eating eggs. The quail egg is much smaller than the chicken egg and the shell is gray with brown spots. The vitamin B₁ content is very high, roughly three times as much as that of a chicken egg. Because it contains less water and has a higher protein content than the chicken eggs, it tastes richer than the latter. Fresh eggs have a lustrous shell and are heavier than old ones, so select them with these points in mind.

Green lettuce leaves are a lovely wrapper for meat, fish and other fillings.

## ☆ HAND-ROLL IN RED LEAF LETTUCE

**RED LEAF LETTUCE**

*SUSHI* RICE

+

Wash and drain

See page 94 ~ 96

### a. ROAST BEEF AND PICKLES ROLL

INGREDIENTS: 4 rolls
4 slices roast beef
4 pickles
A little horseradish sauce

① Cut pickles lengthwise in half.

② Place roast beef on lettuce leaf.

③ Put some horseradish on top.

④ Add pickles.

⑤ Put some *sushi* rice on top.

⑥ Fold up bottom of leaf first. Then fold both sides towards the center.

⑦ It's ready to eat.

## b. CHICKEN *TERIYAKI* ROLL

**INGREDIENTS: 4 rolls**
3 oz. (80 g.) boneless chicken breast, skin removed.
3 Tbsps. *teriyaki* sauce (See page 61)
1²/₅ oz. (40 g.) *kaiwarena*
2 Tbsps. toasted sesame seeds and salt mixture

① Marinate chicken in *teriyaki* sauce for 1 hour. Then broil or grill. Cool and place on lettuce leaf.

② Add *kaiwarena* and sprinkle with toasted sesame seeds and salt mixture. Put *sushi* rice on top.

③ Fold up bottom of leaf first. Then fold both sides towards the center.

## c. ALFALFA SPROUTS, MUSHROOM AND SUNFLOWER SEED ROLL

**INGREDIENTS: 4 rolls**
1³/₅ oz. (40 g.) alfalfa sprouts
4 fresh mushrooms
2 Tbsps. sunflower seeds
2 Tbsps. toasted sesame seed and salt mixture

① Clean mushrooms and slice thin. Place on lettuce leaf.

② Sprinkle with sesame seeds and sunflower seeds and put mushrooms on top. Add *sushi* rice.

③ Fold up bottom of leaf first. Then fold both sides towards the center.

## LETTUCE

Probably native to the Mediterranean region, but now cultivated worldwide, there are three main varieties of lettuce: iceberg lettuce, red leaf lettuce and Boston lettuce. They contain a lot of vitamins and calcium. All three are mainly used raw, in salads, although they can also be cooked or used as a *sushi* ingredient for a change.
They are available year round.

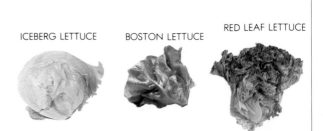

ICEBERG LETTUCE    BOSTON LETTUCE    RED LEAF LETTUCE

★ **Your favorite fresh or cooked foods are arranged on top of the molded *sushi* rice.**

## DIRECTONS:

1 Dip mold in water to prevent sticking.
2 Put rice in mold.
3 Press lightly with back of spoon.
4 Unmold *sushi*.
5 Arrange your favorite food on top.

**b. Ice cream scoop**

**a. Ice cube tray**

**d. Wooden mold**

**c. Cake mold**

# HOW TO SERVE

Serve original *sushi* on a popular morning plate. It's fun and attractive.

# INFORMATION

# ON

# *SUSHI*

# *SUSHI* RICE MAKING

## TYPES OF RICE

There are three main types of rice available; white, short grain Japanese rice, white long grain Chinese rice and instant rice.

The taste and texture of cooked rice depend on the type and quality of the rice, so you should take great care when selecting it. The best rice to buy for *sushi* is white, short grain Japanese rice.

If you are not familiar with rice, go to a well stocked oriental store and buy a package specially marked for *sushi*. If it's not available, the next best is white short grain rice.

If the package is see-through plastic, look for grain that is uniform in size and slightly transparent. Another way to get the best rice is to ask a local *sushi* chef or someone else who would know about *sushi* rice.

## PREPARATION

Rice increases in volume as it cooks, anywhere from two to two and a half times, depending on the kind of rice you use.

If you use a lot of rice, an automatic Japanese rice cooker will make your work a lot easier, so it's a good investment.

However, a Dutch oven or a pot with a fitted lid and good heat distribution will do just as well.

As a general rule equal amounts of rice and water are sufficient for *sushi* rice. But short grain rice grown in California may need a little more water ($\frac{1}{5}$ to $\frac{1}{4}$ cup). For regular unseasoned cooked rice, 1 cup of rice with $1\frac{1}{4}$ cups of water will make moist, fluffy rice. Generally cooking 2 cups of rice is better than cooking 1 cup.

1. Measure rice carefully.
2. Wash rice in a big bowl of water. Rub grains gently; wet grains break easily.
3. Remove any bran or polishing agent. Drain off water well. Repeat this step three more times or until water is almost clear.
4. Leave rice to sit for at least 30 min. in summer and 1 hour in winter. This allows ample time for rice to absorb the water.
5. In cooking pot, mix rice and correct amount of water. Cover with lid.

# SUSHI RICE MAKING

## HOW TO COOK

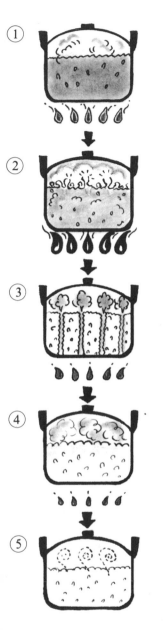

**① • MEDIUM HEAT UNTIL WATER BOILS**
Cook rice over medium heat until water boils. Do not bring it to boiling point quickly. If the quantity of rice is large, cook rice over high heat from the beginning. The heat can be carried into the center of rice if cooked over medium heat.

**② • HIGH HEAT FOR 1 MIN. AFTER BOILING**
When it begins to boil, turn heat to high and cook for 1 min. Never lift lid while cooking. Since the lid might bounce from the pressure of the steam, it is better to place a weight, or some dishes on the lid. Rice absorbs enough water.

**③ • TURN HEAT TO LOW FOR 4-5 MIN.**
Turn heat to low and cook for 4-5 min. (Be careful not to boil over). Then the pot begins to steam. During this interval, there are small holes in rice and steam comes out through these holes.

**④ • THE LOWEST HEAT FOR 10 MIN.**
Reduce heat to the lowest for 10 min.. Every grain of rice absorbs water and becomes plump. It is liable to burn, so cook over the lowest heat.

**⑤ • TURN OFF AND LET RICE STAND FOR 10 MIN.**
Turn off the heat and let rice stand, covered with lid for 10 min. During this 10 min. the grains are allowed to "settle", and the cooking process is completed by the heat retained in the rice and the walls of the pot.

• AUTOMATIC RICE COOKER

Today rice is made daily in practically every Japanese household in an automatic electric or gas rice cooker. The automatic rice cooker, an appliance developed in the postwar period, makes perfect rice. Put washed rice into the cooker, add water. There are measurment marks in the cooker for water and rice volume. Then cover and turn on. Automatic controls take over cooking, reducing heat at exact time, and also in some models, the rice is kept warm till needed. Cookers come in various sizes, from tiny ones holding only a few cups to large ones used in restaurants. Automatic rice cookers, either electric or gas can be obtained at some oriental stores.

# *SUSHI* RICE MAKING

## VINEGAR MIXTURE

| PREPARED *SUSHI* RICE cup | COOKED RICE | | VINEGAR MIXTURE | | |
|---|---|---|---|---|---|
| | Rice cup | Water cup | Vinegar tablespoon (Tbsp.) | Sugar tablespoon (Tbsp.) | Salt teaspoon (tsp.) |
| 2 ½ cups | 1 cup | 1 ⅕ cups | 2 Tbsps. | ½ Tbsp. | 1 tsp. |
| 5 cups | 2 cups | 2 cups | 3 ½ Tbsps. | 1 Tbsp. | 1 ½ tsps. |
| 7 ½ cups | 3 cups | 3-3 ¼ cups * | 5 Tbsps. (⅓ cup) | 1 ½ Tbsps. | 2 tsps. |
| 10 cups | 4 cups | 4-4 ½ cups * | 7 Tbsps. | 2 Tbsps. | 3 tsps. (1 Tbsp.) |

*makes softer rice.

The above proportions are for the basic recipe. The sugar can be increased for a sweeter taste. Ajust the amount of sugar to suit your taste.

## HOW TO TOSS COOKED RICE WITH VINEGAR MIXTURE

Prepare a non-metallic tub, preferably a wooden or a glass (make sure its not polished since the vinegar will remove the wax polish).

① Wash mixing tub well. Dry with kitchen towel.

② Put cooked rice into mixing tub and spread it evenly over the bottom of mixing tub.

③ Sprinkle vinegar mixture generously over the rice. You may not need all of vinegar mixture. Do not add too much liquid.

④ With a large wooden spoon, mix rice by slicing motion.

⑤ All the while you mix, have a helper fan (or electric fan). This is not to cool *sushi* rice, but to puff the extra liquid away.

⑥ Keep *sushi* rice in the wooden tub, covered with a damp cloth.

# FISH

Fresh fish that is eaten raw as *sashimi* and *sushi*, must be prepared from fish that has not been out of the water for more than 24 hours. Also it must be properly chilled. Otherwise most fish has a shelf life of about five days. Of course the ideal fish is that which you catch yourself.

When buying fish, a reliable fish shop can often provide fish of better quality than that found packaged in a supermarket. When buying fish for *sashimi* or *sushi* ask the fishmonger to cut the fish into slices, cubes, whatever you want.

If you are in doubt about the freshness of fish, do not eat it raw. Cook it according to personal preference or marinate it in *teriyaki* sauce and broil. Also no fresh water fish are eaten raw in *sushi* because of the possible presence of parasites. It's similar to eating pork which hasn't been cooked properly. The following are ways to check fish for freshness.

## FRESH FISH

1. Mild characteristic odour, but not too strong or "fishy".
2. Bright, full, clear eyes, not milky or sunken.
3. Bright red gills, not muddy gray, free from slime.
4. Bright characteristic sheen on scales.
5. The scales which are adhering tightly to body, unblemished, without any reddish patches along the ventral area.
6. Firm or rigid body when pressed with fingers.
7. Elastic, firm flesh that does not separate easily from the bones or doesn't indent when handled.
8. Freshly cut appearance with no "leathery" traces of yellowing, browing or drying visible in the flesh.
9. Fresh fish tastes sweet and often has cucumber-like odor.

## FROZEN FISH

1. Solidly frozen package which is tightly wrapped with little or no air space between fish and wrapping. It should be moisture vapour-proofed.
2. Should be kept at a storage temperature below −10°F (−23°C)in the retail food cabinet.
3. There should be no discoloration, fading or drying out evident.

## STORING FISH

1. Since shellfish and fish are the most perishable foods, they should be used as soon as possible.
2. Wash the fish in cold, slightly salty water. Make sure to wash the stomach cavity well. Remove excess moisture with paper towels. Then wrap in waxed paper or freezer wrap. Place in the refrigerator. Handle the fish as little as possible.
3. Frozen fish should be kept frozen solid in freezer wrap or in a suitable container. Do not thaw frozen fish at room temperature before cooking, except when necessary for ease in handling. Thawing frozen fish is best achieved at refrigerator temperature. Once the fish has been thawed out, cook it immediately. Never refreeze fish that has been thawed out. It is advisable not to keep fish frozen for more than three months.
   To remove the odour from utensils, use solution of baking soda and water. (about 1 tsp. soda to a quart of water).

# FISH

To get rid of "fishy" odours on the hands or the chopping board, rub with lemon juice, sliced lemon, vinegar or salt before washing and rinse well. A small amount of toothpaste rubbed on the hands and rinsed off is also a good deodorizer.

Wine, vinegar, ginger, lemon, onion, garlic, in the recipe help to minimize the odour of cooked fish.

## THE NUTRITIONAL VALUE OF FISH

Today Japanese people are the world's leaders where longevity is concerned (in fact number two after Iceland). A lot of the traditional food eaten in Japan came from the sea and still today many varieties of fish are consumed daily. This fact has been linked to "Japanese longevity" and so the fish content of the traditional diet is attracting world wide attention.

It's a well known fact that fish is nutritious. Fresh fish contains a high proportion of protein, and is rich in amino acids, vitamins and fat. All are indispensable for a healthy body. The fat in fish is composed of poly-unsaturated fatty acids and a small amount of cholesterol. The ratio of these contents will vary according to the species. Whatever the ratio, fish contains far less cholesterol and saturated fat than either beef or pork. In fact oily fish like tuna, mackerel, sardine, bonito and horse mackerel are all high in eicosapentaenoic acid. This actually helps to reduce cholesterol and prevents hardening of the arteries.

If you are on a weight reduction diet or a low sodium diet, fish is an ideal food. It should perhaps be noted that salt water fish contain no more sodium than fresh water fish.

## FISH IN SEASON

There was a time when the first foods of any season were ritually offered for the enjoyment of the imperial court. The word for these offerings was *shun*. At the present time the word occurs in a broader context.

The list indicates when typical *sushi* toppings can be expected to taste best in Japan (Tokyo) and on the northeast coast of the United States.

| TOKYO | | NEW YORK | |
|---|---|---|---|
| **SPRING** | | **SPRING** | |
| ark shell | horse mackerel | ark shell | sea urchin |
| cuttlefish | octopus | bonito | soft shell crab |
| flounder | trough shell | fluke | cuttlefish |
| horse clam | sea urchin | horse mackerel | |
| **SUMMER** | | **SUMMER** | |
| abalone | scallop | abalone | sea bass |
| ark shell | sea bass | ark shell | sea urchin |
| prawn | sea urchin | Boston tuna | |
| | | mackerel | |
| **AUTUMN** | | **AUTUMN** | |
| globefish | salmon | Boston tuna | sea bass |
| goby | scallop | mackerel | sea urchin |
| horse clam | sweetfish | | |
| mackerel pike | | | |
| **WINTER** | | **WINTER** | |
| horse clam | tuna | herring | sweet shrimp |
| mackerel | yellowtail | littleneck clam | |
| octopus | | sea urchin | |

# *NORI* SEAWEED

## HOW TO SELECT, HANDLE AND STORE *NORI* SEAWEED

*Nori* seaweed is available in sheets which come in three different sizes.
Large sheet:  $8\frac{1}{4} \times 7\frac{1}{4}$ in. ($21 \times 18$ cm.)
Medium sheet:  $7\frac{1}{4} \times 4\frac{1}{8}$ in. ($10.5 \times 18$ cm.)
Small sheet:  $2\frac{1}{2} \times 2\frac{1}{4}$ in. ($6.5 \times 5.5$ cm.)
Three different types: seasoned, non-seasoned and toasted are available.
Quality *nori* seaweed must be crisp. When buying, look for a well sealed package.

STORAGE:
1. Keep in a cool place, preferably the refrigerator or freezer. Opened packages should be kept in an air-tight container, or wrapped in foil, plastic wrap or freezer wrap to keep out air. Well sealed *nori* seaweed will keep indefinitely in the freezer.
2. Keep in a dark place. Light will affect the flavor of *nori* seaweed.
3. Avoid any moisture.

When *nori* seaweed looses its crispness, lightly toast it over a burner on the lowest setting or preserve it as follow:
Soak *nori* seaweed in a saucepan of hot water. Drain, add soy sauce, *sake* (4 to 1) and simmer over low heat. Add some sugar if you like.

## THE NUTRITIONAL VALUE OF *NORI* SEAWEED

The following are taken from the fourth revised Standard Tables of Food Composition compiled by the Japanese Scientific Research Council in 1982.

Composition of Nutrients in $3\frac{1}{2}$ oz. (100 g.) of *nori* seaweed.

| TYPES OF NORI SEAWEED | Moisture (g.) | Protein (g.) | Fat (g.) | Sugar (g.) | Fiber (g.) | Ash (g.) | Vitamin A (I.U.) | Vitamin $B_1$ (mg.) | Vitamin $B_2$ (mg.) | Vitamin $B_3$ (mg.) | Vitamin C (mg.) |
|---|---|---|---|---|---|---|---|---|---|---|---|
| Dried | 11.1 | 38.8 | 1.9 | 39.5 | 1.8 | 6.9 | 14,000 | 1.15 | 3.40 | 9.8 | 100 |
| Toasted | 6.2 | 40.9 | 2.0 | 41.7 | 1.9 | 7.3 | 13,000 | 1.10 | 3.20 | 9.0 | 95 |
| Seasoned | 4.6 | 38.4 | 2.8 | 39.7 | 1.8 | 12.7 | 12,000 | 1.00 | 2.90 | 8.5 | 75 |

As shown above the protein content is 40%. The nutritional value is equal to that of meat, fish or soy beans. One sheet of *nori* seaweed weighs $\frac{1}{8}$ oz. (3 g.) of which $\frac{1}{25}$ oz. (1.2 g.) is protein. The minimum daily requirement of protein is $2\frac{1}{2}$ oz. (70 g.). *Nori* seaweed itself can't provide essential protein, but it should be noted that it is rich in vitamins A, $B_1$, and $B_2$ is especially high. The table on right-hand side shows a comparison between *nori* seaweed and other foods.
If you are aware of the nutritional value of *nori* seaweed, it will make rolled *sushi* an even more appealing dish. Vinegared rice is rolled in *nori* seaweed using a bamboo mat. something can be put in the center of the rice.

| TYPES OF FOOD | Vitamin A (mg.) | Vitamin $B_1$ (mg.) | Vitamin $B_2$ (mg.) | Vitamin C (mg.) |
|---|---|---|---|---|
| DRIED NORI SEAWEED | 14,000 | 1.15 | 3.40 | 100 |
| WHOLE EGG | 640 | 0.08 | 0.48 | ⊖ |
| FRESH SPINACH | 1,700 | 0.13 | 0.23 | 65 |
| MILK | 110 | 0.03 | 0.15 | ⊖ |

# GLOSSARY

## ABURAGE

Deep fried *tofu*. Before frying, it is cut into thin slices, and fried until out-side becomes crisp.

## ASATSUKI

*Asatsuki* is a kind of green onion. It is used as a garnishing for *sushi*.

## DAIKON RADISH

*Daikon* radish is rich in vitamins, and its leaves contain a lot of calcium. This radish is thought to aid in digesting oily foods. It is good for simmered dishes.

## DASHI STOCK

*Dashi* stock is Japanese clear soup stock. There are four types made from kelp, dried bonito, *shiitake* mushroom, or dried fish. *Dashi* stock is the secret of Japanese cooking.

## FREEZE DRIED *TOFU*

This is made from soy beans. One package usually contains 5 to 6 pieces. It looks like a beige sponge and is very light. Prior to cooking, it should be soaked in luke warm water until soft. It will double in volume. It is easily simmered and it goes well with soy sauce. Freeze dried *tofu* was originally a daily food for monks in Japan. Now it is popular among people.

## GINGER ROOT

Choose ginger root that is firm and tight. Avoid pieces that are flabby or have soft spots. Pare skin of amount you will use.

## KAIWARENA

*Kaiwarena* is the *daikon* radish sprout. Like *daikon* radish, it contains lots of vitamins and minerals.

## KAMPYO

*Kampyo* is dried gourd shavings. It is used as one of the fillings for rolled *sushi*. To soften, first wash and then knead the required amount in ample salt. Wash in water, boil until soft. It is available in 1oz. (30g.) packets.

## LOTUS ROOT

The flesh is white and "crunchy". Long tubular hollows run through the entire length of the root. When preparing lotus root for cooking, pare it first. Then cut into rounds. The shape should be attractive. To prevent discoloring it should be immersed for a short time in a mixture of alum and water or

vinegar and water. This also gets rid of any harshness in flavor. It can then be boiled in water containing a little vinegar. It goes well with vinegared dishes.

## MIRIN

*Mirin* is heavily sweetened *sake*, used for cooking. *Mirin* is also called "sweet cooking rice wine." It adds aroma and a touch of sweetness and is a basic seasoning in Japanese cooking.

# GLOSSARY

## NATTO

This is a fermented soy bean preparation made by the action of special bacteria. It has a rich cheese-like flavor and is sticky. With good *natto*, sticky threads when mixing.

## PICKLED PLUM PASTE

Green plums and red *shiso* leaves are salted and pickled together. The leaves provide the flavor and the color. The paste itself tastes the same as pickled plum.

## RICE

The rice that is prefered by Japanese people is short-grain rice. Short-grain rice is some what sticker and moister than long-grain rice. The rice that Japanese people prefer is quite different from the one Western people think good. People in the West think rice should be dry and not sticky. The rice, which is dry like long-grain rice is not appropriate for Japanese cuisine, and should be avoided. Short-grain rice is always available in oriental food stores. (See page 94-96)

## RICE VINEGAR

Japanese produce various kinds of rice vinegar, but every type is still milder than most Western vinegars. Lightness and light sweetness are the characteristics of Japanese rice vinegar. Japanese rice vinegar is one of the most important ingredients of *sushi*. It goes well with rice and raw fish. If you substitute, use cider vinegar.

## SAKE

*Sake* is the most popular, ancient beverage in Japan. *Sake* is made by inoculating steamed malt (*koji*), allowing fermentation to occur, and then refining. There are three grades of *sake*. They are special class, first class, and second class. Also *sake* can be divided into sweet types and "dry" types in taste. Sometimes Japanese drink it cold, but it is usually warmed befor drinking. For "dry" *sake*, the temperature should be 108-113°F (42-45°C), and for sweet *sake*, 113-122°F (45-50°C).
*Sake* is not only for drinking. It is used as a seasoning in Japanese cooking.

## SESAME SEEDS

Both black and white sesame seeds are used in Japanese cooking. When toasted sesame seeds have a much richer aroma and flavor. Richer still however, are ground sesame seeds. To grind sesame seeds, first toast them in a dry frying pan. Then put into a *suribachi* (Japanese grinding bowl), and grind. It should be a nice garnishing.

## SHIITAKE MUSHROOM

Both fresh and dried *shiitake* mushrooms can be obtained. Dried ones should be soaked in water before using. This soaking water makes *dashi* stock (Japanese soup stock). Fresh *shiitake* mushroom have a distinctive, appealing "woodsy-fruity" flavor. *Shiitake* mushroom is good for simmered dishes with its excellent flavor. The best ones have thick, brown velvety caps, and firm flesh.

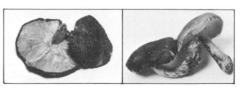

# GLOSSARY

## *SHISO* LEAVES

These minty, aromatic leaves come in green and red varieties. The red type is used to make *umeboshi* (pickled plum).

## SOY SAUCE

Soy sauce is made from soy beans, and salt. It is the primary seasoning in Japanese cooking. It is used for simmered foods, dressings, soups-many kinds of Japanese dishes. There are two kinds of soy sauce. One is ordinary soy sauce and the other is light soy sauce. Light soy sauce has a light color and is salty enough. It does not darken the color of the foods.

Soy sauce gives a delicate flavor and taste to foods. Especially for *sushi*, there is no other seasoning but soy sauce. It goes well with ginger root and also *wasabi*. Soy sauce is the essence of Japanese cuisine.

## *TEMAKI KATSUO* SHEET

These are shaved bonito flakes which have been pressed and cut into three different size. It is available in four different flavors.

## TREFOIL

Trefoil is a member of the parsley family. The flavor is somewhere between sorrel and celery. The color of trefoil is light green and attractive. It is used in many Japanese dishes as a flavor and color accent. The leaves lose their fragrance easily so do not simmer too long or subjected to too much heat.

## *WASABI*

*Wasabi* is Japanese horseradish. It is pale green in color. It has a more delicate aroma and is milder tasting than Western horseradish. In Japan both fresh and powdered *wasabi* are available, but it is hard to obtain fresh *wasabi* in other countries. The edible part of *wasabi* is the root. Usually it comes in powdered form or in a tube, but the fragrant of fresh *wasabi* is much richer than powdered *wasabi*. The powder should be mixed with water to make thick paste. *Wasabi* accompanies most raw fish dishes, and also *sushi*. Raw fish may be hard to try for the first time, but with the taste of soy sauce and *wasabi*, it must soon be one of your favorites.

Japanese foods sponsored by Nishimoto Trading Co., Ltd.

# GLOSSARY

## BAMBOO MAT [*makisu*]

The bamboo mat is used for rolling *sushi*. It is made of narrow strips of bamboo bound with strong cotton. Three sizes are available.

Large:   $12 \times 10\frac{3}{4}$ in. ($30 \times 27$ cm.)
Medium:  $10\frac{3}{4} \times 9\frac{3}{4}$ in. ($27 \times 25$ cm.)
Small:   $9\frac{3}{4} \times 9\frac{1}{2}$ in. ($25 \times 26.5$ cm.)

It is not necessary to buy all three; the large one is most versatile. After using the bamboo mat, wash it under tepid, running water and wipe off. Let it dry compeletly before putting it away.

HOW TO USE BAMBOO MAT

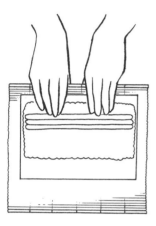 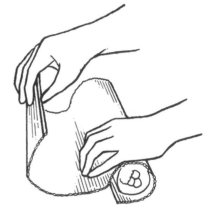

① Place *nori* seaweed on bamboo mat then the rice and fillings as illustrated. Lift front end of the bamboo mat with thumbs. Press rice slightly with rest of fingers.

② Roll everything together in the direction of the far end of the bamboo mat. Press slightly.

③ Adjust the form of the rolled *sushi* by squeezing it gently and carefully.

## MIXING TUB [*hangiri*]

This is used for mixing the cooked rice with the vinegar flavoring. In *sushi* shops a cypress tub is used. However, a large, plastic or enamel or glass bowl will do just as well.

## WOODEN MOLD [*oshiwaku*]

This wooden mold is used to make pressed *sushi*. The mold consists of three pieces. It looks like a large oriental puzzle. If you make *sushi* often, the wooden mold is useful, but it is not essential. Instead of the mold, you can use a pan with a removable bottom, a stainless spring-form pan, or, if you have utensils for French cooking, you can innovate with a stainless form pans.

# SPECIAL TERMS USED IN *SUSHI* RESTAURANTS

The *sushi* shop can be an interesting language experience. Even the person who understands Japanese may be baffled when he first hears the words spoken by the *sushi* chef and his helpers, for they have their own jargon.
The following are a short selection of traditional terms.

**Agari** (ah-ga-ri)
> Hot green tea. Usually *ocha*. *Agari,* signifying that a person has finished eating. Originally *agari* meant only the cup of tea served after meal, but now whenever.

**Ebi** (eh-bi)
> Prawn. It is one of the most popular ingredients of *sushi*. Prawn which is served alive is called *odori-ebi* (dancing prawn).

**Gari** (ga-ri)
> Vinegar pickled ginger root. Thinly sliced and always served with *sushi*. Taken between bites, it freshens the palate so you can savor the unique taste of each *sushi*.

**Geso** (ge-so)
> Cuttlefish tentacles. Cooked and used for *sushi* as a topping. *Sushi* with *geso* is seasoned with thick sauce and served.

**Hikari-mono** (hi-ka-ri mo-no)
> Fish that have shiny skin. *Aji* (horse mackerel), *kohada* (gizzard shad), mackerel, halfbeak, sea bream or sillago. Usually vinegared and put on top of *sushi*.

**Ichinin-mae** (ichi-ni-n ma-e)
> A serving for one person. The word is used to order the thick omelet eaten at the end of a meal of *sushi*.

**Kappa** (ka-pa)
> Rolled *sushi* with Japanese cucumber.

**Murasaki** (mu-ra-sa-ki)
> Soy sauce. Usually, *shoyu*. It is neccessary for *sushi* as dipping sauce.

**Naka-ochi** (na-ka o-chi)
> Rolled *sushi* with filling of finely chopped tuna.

**Oaiso** (o-a-i-so)
> Bill or check.

**Oshinko** (o-shin-ko)
> Pale yellow pickled *daikon* radish.

**Otemoto** (o-te-mo-to)
> Chopsticks. Usually called *hashi*.

**Sabi** (sa-bi)
> *Wasabi*. Japanese horseradish.

**Shari** (sha-ri)
> *Sushi* rice. *Shari* comes from a Sanskrit word.

**Shitadai** (shi-ta-da-i)
> Menu. Ordinary *shitadai* means a prologue of a play.

**Tekka** (tet-ka)
> Rolled *sushi* with tuna.

# HOW TO EAT *SUSHI*

After *nigiri-zushi* was created, some thought was given to convenient and appetizing ways of eating it. The preferred ways, using either the fingers or chopsticks, are described below.

## USE FINGERS

To eat *sushi* with the fingers:

  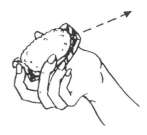

① Place the forefinger on topping of *nigiri-zushi* first and pick up the piece with the thumb and middle finger.

② Dip topping in soy sauce. Or turn the piece of *nigiri-zushi* up-side-down and dip the end of topping in soy sauce.

③ Place the *sushi* in the mouth so that the topping encounters the tongue first.

Fondness for soy sauce leads some people to soak the rice part of *sushi* in this seasoning. This is not recommended, since, not only will the rice fall apart, but the flavors of both topping and rice will be obliterated. Soy sauce should complement, not conceal, the foods it is eaten with.

## USE CHOPSTICKS

The chopsticks may be joined at the top. Carefully split them apart.
1. Place one chopstick in the hollow between the thumb and forefinger and support it on the ring finger.
2. Hold the other chopstick with the tips of the thumb, forefinger and middle finger and manipulate its tip against the tip of the other one, which is held stationary.

To eat *sushi* with chopsticks:

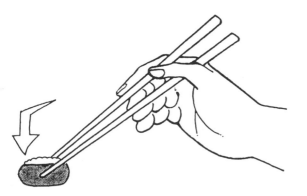 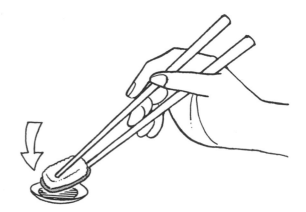

① Turn the *sushi* on one side gently, so that the rice doesn't fall apart.

② Dip the end of the topping in soy sauce. Convey the *sushi* to the mouth with the side facing down.

# METRIC TABLES

Today many areas of the world use the metric system and more will follow in the future. The following tables are conversion tables for those who need them in their cooking.

## Liquid Measures

| U.S. Customary system | oz. | g. | ml. |
|---|---|---|---|
| 1/16 cup = 1 T. | 1/2 oz. | 14 g. | 15 ml. |
| 1/4 cup = 4 T. | 2 oz. | 60 g. | 59 ml. |
| 1/2 cup = 8 T. | 4 oz. | 115 g. | 118 ml. |
| 1 cup = 16 T. | 8 oz. | 225 g. | 236 ml. |
| 1 3/4 cups | 14 oz. | 400 g. | 414 ml. |
| 2 cups = 1 pint | 16 oz. | 450 g. | 473 ml. |
| 3 cups | 24 oz. | 685 g. | 710 ml. |
| 4 cups | 32 oz. | 900 g. | 946 ml. |

General points of information that may prove valuable or of interest:

1 British fluid of ounce = 28.5 ml.
1 American fluid ounce = 29.5 ml.

1 Japanese cup = 200 ml.
1 British cup = 200 ml. = 7 British fl oz.
1 American cup = 240 ml. = 8 American fl oz.

1 British pint = 570 ml. = 20 British fl oz.
1 American pint = 470 ml. = 16 American fl oz.

T. = tablespoon  oz. = ounce  g. = gram  ml. = milliliter

## Weights

| grams to ounces | | ounces to grams* | |
|---|---|---|---|
| 1 g. = 0.035 oz. | | 1/4 oz. = 7 g. | |
| 5 g. = 1/6 oz. | | 1/2 oz. = 14 g. | |
| 10 g. = 1/3 oz. | | 1 oz. = 30 g. | |
| 30 g. = 1 oz. | | 2 oz. = 60 g. | |
| 100 g. = 3 1/2 oz. | | 4 oz. = 115 g. | |
| 200 g. = 7 oz. | | 6 oz. = 170 g. | |
| 500 g. = 18 oz. | | 8 oz. = 225 g. | |
| 1000 g. = 35 oz. | | 16 oz. = 450 g. | |

grams × 0.035 = ounces
ounces × 28.35 = grams

*Equivalent

## Linear Measures

| inches to centimeters | centimeters to inches* |
|---|---|
| 1/2 in. = 1.27 cm. | 1 cm. = 3/8 in. |
| 1 in. = 2.54 cm. | 2 cm. = 3/4 in. |
| 2 in. = 5.08 cm. | 3 cm. = 1 1/6 in. |
| 4 in. = 10.16 cm. | 4 cm. = 1 1/2 in. |
| 5 in. = 12.7 cm. | 5 cm. = 2 in. |
| 10 in. = 25.4 cm. | 10 cm. = 4 in. |
| 15 in. = 38.1 cm. | 15 cm. = 5 3/4 in. |
| 20 in. = 50.8 cm. | 20 cm. = 8 in. |

inches × 2.54 = centimeters
centimeters × 0.39 = inches

in. = inch  cm. = centimeter

## Temperatures

| Fahrenheit (F.) to Celsius (C.) | | Celsius (C.) to Fahrenheit (F.) | |
|---|---|---|---|
| freezer storage | −10F. = −23.3C. | freezer storage | −20C. = −4F. |
| | 0F. = −17.7C. | | −10C. = 14F. |
| water freezes | 32F. = 0 C. | water freezes | 0C. = 32F. |
| | 68F. = 20 C. | | 10C. = 50F. |
| | 100F. = 37.7C. | | 50C. = 122F. |
| water boils | 212F. = 100 C. | water boils | 100C. = 212F. |
| | 300F. = 148.8C. | | 150C. = 302F. |
| | 400F. = 204.4C. | | 200C. = 392F. |

The water boiling temperature given is at sea level.

Conversion factors:
$$C. = F. - 32 \times \tfrac{5}{9}$$
$$F. = \frac{C. \times 9}{5} + 32$$

C. = Celsius   F. = Fahrenheit

# INDEX